Recipes: The Cooking of Provincial France

Contents

Hors d'Oeuvre 2

Soups 17

Fish 30

Poultry 41

Meat... 54

Vegetables 84

Desserts 96

Index.. 109

Foods of the World

TIME-LIFE BOOKS, NEW YORK

Hors d'Oeuvre

Saucisson en Croûte
SAUSAGE BAKED IN PASTRY CRUST

To serve 4 to 6

1½- to 2-pound uncooked plain or garlic pork sausage, about 12 inches long and 2 inches in diameter, fresh or smoked (French, Italian or Polish)
Water
Pâte brisée (page 4)
1 egg beaten with 1 teaspoon water
Dijon-style prepared mustard

With the point of a sharp knife, prick the sausage in 5 or 6 places to prevent the skin from bursting, and to release its fat when it cooks. Lay the sausage flat in a large, deep skillet and add enough cold water to cover it completely. Bring to a boil over moderate heat and simmer uncovered for 45 minutes. Transfer the sausage to paper towels to drain and cool. Then split the skin with a sharp knife and peel it off.

Preheat the oven to 375°. Roll the *pâte brisée* out ⅛ inch thick in a rectangular shape large enough to wrap around the sausage (about 8 inches long and 15 inches wide). Center the cooled sausage on the rectangle. Cut triangles of pastry from each corner of the roll and gently, without stretching the dough, lift the long sides of the pastry up over the sausage. The pastry should overlap by about an inch on top; trim off anything more than that with a knife. Brush the lower edge of the pastry with the egg-water mixture and press the upper edge down upon it firmly to secure it.

Brush the envelopelike flaps at the ends of the roll with a little egg mixture, then lift the flaps up over the ends of the sausage and tuck the edges in neatly to seal them. Turn the wrapped sausage over and place it seam-side down on a buttered baking sheet. Cut the pastry scraps into decorative shapes such as half moons, diamonds or leaves and arrange these on top of the roll, sealing them in place with the egg-water mixture. With a pastry brush, coat the whole roll with the rest of the egg mixture. Bake the roll on the middle shelf of the oven for 45 to 60 minutes or until it is golden brown. Transfer the roll to a large platter and serve it cut into ¾-inch slices. Pass the mustard separately.

Fondue de Fromage

CHEESE FONDUE, FRENCH STYLE

To serve 6 to 8

2 cups dry white wine
2 garlic cloves, cut up
¾ pound imported Swiss cheese,
    freshly grated (about 3 cups)
    mixed with 1 tablespoon cornstarch

2 tablespoons butter
2 to 6 tablespoons heavy cream
Salt
Freshly ground black pepper
3 tablespoons kirsch
1 loaf French or Italian bread cut
    in 1-inch cubes

In a 1½- to 2-quart saucepan, boil the wine and garlic briskly until the wine has reduced to 1½ cups. Strain the reduced wine through a fine sieve into a fondue pot or the cooking pan of a chafing dish that has a lower pan to fill with water; discard the garlic. At the table or in the kitchen, light the burner under the fondue pot or the chafing dish pan. Over direct heat, return the wine to a boil, then lower the heat at once and add the cheese-cornstarch mixture, stirring constantly with a table fork. Do not let this mixture boil; if it seems to be getting too hot, lift the pan off the heat for a few seconds to cool it. When all the cheese has melted and the fondue is smooth, stir in the butter and 2 tablespoons of cream. The fondue should be just thick enough to coat the fork heavily. If it seems too thick, add a little more cream, 1 tablespoon at a time. Season it with a little salt and pepper, stir in the kirsch, and serve at once, accompanied by a platter of bread cubes. If you are using a chafing dish, set the pan over hot water to keep the fondue warm.

To eat the fondue, spear a bread cube with a fork, dip the bread into the hot cheese and twirl the bread to coat it evenly with fondue. If the fondue should thicken while you are eating it, heat a little cream and stir it in to thin it.

ALTERNATIVE: The traditional Swiss fondue is similar, but simpler, and does not include any butter or cream. To make it, bring the wine and garlic to a boil in the fondue pot or chafing dish and let them cook for a minute or so, but do not boil down the wine. Remove the garlic and add the cheese a handful at a time. When all the cheese is added and the mixture is smooth and creamy, season the fondue with salt and pepper, and stir in the kirsch.

Quiche au Fromage
OPEN-FACED CHEESE TART

To make an 8- to 9-inch *quiche*

PÂTE BRISÉE (pastry dough or pie
  crust)
6 tablespoons chilled butter,
  cut in ¼-inch bits

2 tablespoons chilled vegetable
  shortening
1½ cups all-purpose flour
¼ teaspoon salt
3 to 5 tablespoons ice water

PÂTE BRISÉE: In a large, chilled mixing bowl, combine butter, vegetable shortening, flour and salt. Working quickly, use your fingertips to rub the flour and fat together until they blend and look like flakes of coarse meal. Pour 3 tablespoons of ice water over the mixture all at once, toss together lightly and gather the dough into a ball. If the dough seems crumbly, add up to 2 tablespoons more ice water by drops. Dust the pastry with a little flour and wrap it in wax paper or a plastic bag. Refrigerate it for at least 3 hours or until it is firm.

Remove the pastry from the refrigerator 5 minutes before rolling it. If it seems resistant and hard, tap it all over with a rolling pin. Place the ball on a floured board or table and, with the heel of one hand, press it into a flat circle about 1 inch thick. Dust a little flour over and under it and roll it out—from the center to within an inch of the far edge. Lift the dough and turn it clockwise, about the space of two hours on a clock; roll again from the center to the far edge. Repeat—lifting, turning, rolling—until the circle is about ⅛ inch thick and 11 or 12 inches across. If the pastry sticks to the board or table, lift it gently with a metal spatula and sprinkle a little flour under it.

Butter the bottom and sides of an 8- to 9-inch false-bottomed *quiche* or cake pan no more than 1¼ inches deep. Roll the pastry over the pin and unroll it over the pan, or drape the pastry over the rolling pin, lift it up and unfold it over the pan. Gently press the pastry into the bottom and around the sides of the pan, being careful not to stretch it. Roll the pin over the rim of the pan, pressing down hard to trim off the excess pastry. With a fork, prick the bottom of the pastry all over, trying not to pierce all the way through. Chill for 1 hour.

Preheat the oven to 400°. To keep the bottom of the pastry from puffing up, spread a sheet of buttered aluminum foil across the pan and press it gently into the edges to support the sides of the pastry as it bakes. Bake on the middle shelf of the oven for 10 minutes, then remove the foil. Prick the pastry again, then return it to the oven for 3 minutes or until it starts to shrink from the sides of the pan and begins to brown. Remove it from the oven and set it on a wire cake rack to cool.

CHEESE-CUSTARD FILLING

1 teaspoon butter
6 slices lean bacon, cut in ¼-inch
    pieces
2 eggs plus 2 extra egg yolks
1½ cups heavy cream
½ teaspoon salt

Pinch of white pepper
¾ cup grated imported Swiss cheese or
    Swiss and freshly grated Parmesan
    cheese combined
2 tablespoons butter, cut in tiny
    pieces

CHEESE-CUSTARD FILLING: Preheat the oven to 375°. In a heavy 8- to 10-inch skillet, melt the butter over moderate heat. When the foam subsides, cook the bacon until it is lightly browned and crisp. Remove from the skillet with a slotted spoon and drain on paper towels. With a wire whisk, rotary or electric beater, beat the eggs, extra egg yolks, cream and seasonings together in a large mixing bowl. Stir in the grated cheese. Place the cooled pastry shell on a baking sheet. Scatter the bacon over the bottom of the shell and gently ladle the egg-cheese custard into it, being sure the custard does not come within ⅛ inch of the rim of the shell. Sprinkle the top with dots of butter and bake in the upper third of the oven for 25 minutes or until the custard has puffed and browned and a knife inserted in the center comes out clean. To remove the *quiche* from the pan, set the pan on a large jar or coffee can and slip down the outside rim. Run a long metal spatula under the *quiche* to make sure it isn't stuck to the bottom of the pan, then slide the *quiche* onto a heated platter. Serve hot or warm.

Salade Niçoise
MEDITERRANEAN VEGETABLE SALAD

To serve 4 to 6

1 large head Boston or romaine lettuce,
    separated, washed and dried
1 to 2 cups French potato salad *(page 12)*
4 large, firm ripe tomatoes,
    quartered
3 hard-cooked eggs, cooled, peeled
    and quartered
1 seven-ounce can tuna fish (preferably

packed in olive oil), drained and
    broken in chunks
½ cup black olives (Mediterranean
    style, if possible), drained
8 to 12 flat anchovy fillets, drained
2 cups blanched green string beans,
    chilled *(page 89)*
½ cup *sauce vinaigrette (page 16)*
3 tablespoons finely chopped fresh
    parsley

Line a large salad bowl—preferably a glass one—with the lettuce, and spread the potato salad in the bottom of the bowl. Arrange the tomato quarters, egg quarters, tuna chunks, olives, anchovies and green beans on top in an attractive pattern—concentric circles, wedges or strips. Spoon the *vinaigrette* over the salad, sprinkle with parsley and serve immediately.

Soufflé au Fromage

CHEESE SOUFFLÉ

To serve 4

1 tablespoon soft butter
1 tablespoon grated, imported Swiss
  cheese
3 tablespoons butter
3 tablespoons flour
1 cup hot milk

½ teaspoon salt
Pinch of white pepper
4 egg yolks
6 egg whites
1 cup grated, imported Swiss cheese
  or ½ cup each Swiss and freshly
  grated Parmesan cheese

Preheat the oven to 400°. Grease the bottom and sides of a 2-quart French soufflé dish or charlotte mold with 1 tablespoon of soft butter, then sprinkle in 1 tablespoon of grated imported Swiss cheese, tipping the dish to spread the cheese as evenly as possible on the bottom and on all sides. Set the dish aside.

In a 2- to 3-quart saucepan, melt 3 tablespoons butter over moderate heat. When the foam subsides, stir in the 3 tablespoons of flour with a wooden spoon and cook over low heat, stirring constantly for 1 or 2 minutes. Do not let the *roux* (the butter and flour mixture) brown. Remove the saucepan from the heat and pour in the hot milk, beating vigorously with a whisk until the *roux* and liquid are blended. Add the salt and pepper and return to low heat and cook, whisking constantly, until the sauce comes to a boil and is smooth and thick. Let it simmer a moment, then remove the pan from the heat and beat in the egg yolks, one at a time, whisking until each one is thoroughly blended before adding the next. Set aside.

With a large balloon whisk, beat the egg whites until they are so stiff that they form small points which stand straight up without wavering. (A rotary or electric beater may be used instead, but the whites will not mount as voluminously or have as fine a texture.) Stir a big spoonful of beaten egg white into the waiting sauce to lighten it; then stir in all but 1 tablespoon of the remaining grated cheese. With a spatula, lightly fold in the rest of the egg whites, using an over-under cutting motion rather than a stirring motion.

Gently pour the soufflé mixture into the prepared dish; the dish should be about three quarters full. Lightly smooth the surface with a rubber spatula and sprinkle the remaining tablespoonful of cheese on top. For a decorative effect make a "cap" on the soufflé with a spatula by cutting a trench about 1 inch deep and 1 inch from the rim all around the dish. Place the soufflé on the middle shelf of the oven and immediately turn the heat down to 375°. Bake for 25 to 30 minutes, or until the soufflé puffs up about 2 inches above the rim of the dish and the top is lightly browned. Serve at once.

SOUFFLÉ AU FROMAGE ET AUX OEUFS MOLLETS (cheese soufflé with boiled eggs): Bring 2 quarts of water to a boil in a heavy 3- to 4-quart saucepan. Lower 4 eggs into the water and boil them slowly for 6 minutes (boil them for 7 minutes if they have been refrigerated). Drain immediately and run cold water into the pan. Tap the eggs gently on a hard surface to break their shells, and peel them under a stream of cold water. Preheat the oven to 400°. Prepare the soufflé mixture, following the directions in the recipe above. Scoop about half of it into a buttered and cheese-lined 2-quart French soufflé dish or charlotte mold. Arrange the eggs in a circle on top and cover each with a mound of the remaining soufflé mixture. Dot each mound with a teaspoon of grated cheese and place the soufflé on the middle shelf of the oven. Immediately turn the heat down to 375° and bake for 25 to 30 minutes. When you serve the soufflé, include an egg in each portion.

Anchoyade
HOT ANCHOVY CANAPÉ

To serve 4 to 5

2 two-ounce cans flat anchovy fillets	Freshly ground black pepper
2 medium garlic cloves, finely chopped	8 to 10 slices fresh French bread
1 teaspoon tomato paste	(½- to ¾-inch slices)
1 to 1½ tablespoons olive oil	1 teaspoon finely chopped fresh
2 teaspoons lemon juice or red-wine vinegar	parsley

Drain the anchovies of all their oil and place them in a large mortar or heavy bowl with the garlic and the tomato paste. Mash with a pestle, wooden masher or wooden spoon until the mixture is a very smooth purée. Dribble the oil in, a few drops at a time, stirring constantly, until the mixture becomes thick and smooth like mayonnaise. Stir in the lemon juice and a few grindings of pepper.

Preheat the oven to 500°. Under the broiler, brown the bread lightly on one side. While the bread is warm, spread the untoasted, soft side with the anchovy mixture, pressing it into the bread with the back of a fork or spoon. Arrange the bread on a baking sheet and bake in the oven for 10 minutes. Sprinkle with parsley and serve at once.

NOTE: For less saltiness, after draining the anchovies soak them for 10 minutes in cold water and then pat them thoroughly dry with paper towels.

Légumes à la Grecque

MARINATED VEGETABLES, GREEK STYLE

To serve 8 to 10

MARINADE
3 cups chicken stock, fresh or canned
1 cup dry white wine
1 cup olive oil

½ cup lemon juice
6 parsley sprigs
2 large garlic cloves, cut up
½ teaspoon dried thyme
10 peppercorns
1 teaspoon salt

First make the marinade. Stir the ingredients together in a 3- to 4-quart enameled or stainless-steel saucepan, bring to a boil, partially cover the pan and simmer slowly for 45 minutes. Using a fine sieve, strain the marinade into a large bowl, pressing down hard on the ingredients with the back of a spoon to squeeze out their juices before discarding them. Return the marinade to the saucepan and taste it. To be effective, the marinade should be somewhat overseasoned. This makes about 5 cups.

VEGETABLES
24 white onions, 1 inch in diameter, peeled
1 pound small zucchini, unpeeled, sliced 1 inch thick
1 pound small yellow squash,

unpeeled, sliced 1 inch thick
3 medium green peppers, seeded and cut lengthwise into ½-inch strips
½ pound whole green string beans, trimmed
2 lemons, cut into ¼-inch slices

Bring the marinade to a boil and add the onions; cover and cook over moderate heat for 20 to 30 minutes or until the onions are just tender when pierced with the tip of a sharp knife. With a slotted spoon, remove the onions to a large glass or stainless-steel baking dish.

Add the slices of zucchini and yellow squash to the simmering marinade and cook slowly uncovered for 10 to 15 minutes or until they are barely done, then put them in the baking dish with the onions. Finally, add the green-pepper strips and string beans to the marinade and cook them slowly uncovered for 8 to 10 minutes, or until they are just tender. The vegetables must not be overcooked because they will soften as they cool and marinate. Lift the green peppers and string beans out of the pan and add them to the other vegetables. Taste and season the marinade and pour it over the vegetables, making sure that they are all at least partly covered with the hot liquid.

Place the baking dish in the refrigerator to cool the vegetables. Then cover the dish tightly with aluminum foil or plastic wrap and let the vegetables marinate in the refrigerator for at least 4 hours—or overnight if possible—before serving them. To serve, lift the vegetables out of the marinade with a slotted spoon and arrange them attractively on a serving platter. Moisten the vegetables with a little marinade and garnish them with lemon slices.

NOTE: Any other firm vegetable may be added to or substituted for those in the recipe, such as mushrooms, celery hearts, leeks, cucumbers, red peppers and artichoke hearts.

Pipérade
OPEN-FACED OMELET WITH PEPPERS, TOMATOES AND HAM

To serve 4

1/4 cup olive oil
1/2 cup finely chopped onions
  or scallions
1 small garlic clove, finely chopped
2 small green peppers, seeded and cut
  in 1- by 1/2-inch strips (about 3/4 cup)
1 pound firm, ripe tomatoes, peeled,
  seeded and coarsely chopped (about
  1 1/2 cups)
2 teaspoons finely chopped fresh basil

or 1 teaspoon dried basil, crumbled
1/8 teaspoon Tabasco
1 tablespoon olive oil
1 tablespoon butter
1/4 pound smoked cooked ham cut in
  1- by 1/2-inch julienne strips (about
  1 cup)
6 to 8 eggs, lightly beaten
Salt
Freshly ground black pepper
1 tablespoon finely chopped fresh
  parsley

In a heavy 8- to 10-inch skillet, heat 1/4 cup of oil. When the oil is very hot, stir in the onions and garlic, and cook over moderate heat, stirring frequently, for 5 minutes, or until they are soft but not browned. Stir in the green-pepper strips and cook, stirring occasionally, for 8 to 10 minutes, or until the peppers are barely tender. Drain the tomatoes and stir them into the skillet along with the basil and Tabasco. Increase the heat and cook, stirring constantly, for 2 or 3 minutes or until most of the liquid has evaporated. Cover the skillet lightly to keep the *pipérade* mixture warm and set aside.

In an 8-inch serving skillet or a shallow, flameproof serving dish, heat 1 tablespoon each of oil and butter. When the foam subsides, stir in the ham and cook over moderate heat for a few minutes to warm it through. Remove the ham with a slotted spoon and drain it on paper towels. Remove the skillet from the heat and let the fat cool to lukewarm. In a small bowl, beat the eggs with a fork or whisk until they are well blended, then season with salt and pepper. Return the skillet to low heat and pour in the eggs. Stirring with the flat of a table fork or a rubber spatula, cook the eggs until they begin to form soft, creamy curds. Gently spread the warm *pipérade* mixture over them, mixing some of the vegetables into the eggs. Scatter the ham on top, sprinkle with parsley, and serve at once.

Crêpes Fourrées Gratinées

FILLED FRENCH PANCAKES

To make 16 stuffed *crêpes*

CRÊPES
1¼ cups all-purpose flour
3 eggs
1 cup milk

¼ cup water
½ teaspoon salt
3 tablespoons butter, melted and
   cooled
3 tablespoons melted butter combined
   with 1 tablespoon vegetable oil

THE CRÊPES: To make the batter in a blender combine flour, eggs, milk, water, salt and 3 tablespoons melted butter in the blender jar and blend them at high speed for a few seconds. Turn the machine off, scrape down the sides of the jar and blend again for 40 seconds. To make the batter by hand, stir the flour and eggs together in a mixing bowl and gradually stir in the milk, water and salt. Beat with a whisk or rotary or electric beater until the flour lumps disappear, then force through a fine sieve into another bowl and stir in 3 tablespoons of melted butter. The batter should be the consistency of heavy cream; dilute it if necessary by beating in cold water a teaspoon at a time. In either case, refrigerate the batter in the blender jar or bowl for an hour or two before using it.

Now heat a 6-inch *crêpe* pan or skillet over high heat until a drop of water flicked into it evaporates instantly. With a pastry brush, lightly grease the bottom and sides of the pan with a little of the melted butter and oil combination. With a small ladle pour about 2 tablespoons of batter into the pan and tip the pan so that the batter quickly covers the bottom; the batter should cling to the pan and begin to firm up almost immediately. At once tilt the pan over the bowl and pour off any excess batter; the finished *crêpe* should be paper thin. Cook the *crêpe* for a minute or so until a rim of brown shows around the edge. Turn it over with a spatula and cook the other side for a minute longer. Slide the *crêpe* onto a plate. Brush butter and oil on the skillet again and proceed with the rest of the *crêpes*. The *crêpes* should be no more than 1/16 inch thick. Dilute the batter by beating in drops of water if necessary. *Crêpes* may be made hours or even days ahead of time and kept, tightly covered, in the refrigerator or freezer. If you do this, let them return to room temperature before attempting to separate them.

DUXELLES
¾ pound fresh mushrooms, finely
   chopped (about 3 cups)
4 tablespoons butter
4 tablespoons finely chopped
   shallots or scallions

1 teaspoon finely chopped fresh
   parsley
1 teaspoon finely cut fresh chives
Salt
Freshly ground black pepper

DUXELLES: A handful at a time, place the chopped mushrooms in the corner of a towel and squeeze to extract as much juice as possible. In a heavy 8- to 10-inch skillet, melt 4 tablespoons of butter over moderate heat. Before the foam subsides, stir in the shallots and cook them, stirring constantly, for 1 or 2 minutes or until they are soft but not brown. Stir in the squeezed, chopped mushrooms and cook, stirring frequently, for 10 to 15 minutes or until the moisture they give off has evaporated and they are on the point of browning. Transfer them to a bowl and stir in the parsley and chives. Season with salt and pepper. This makes about 1 cup.

VELOUTÉ SAUCE	
6 tablespoons butter	2 egg yolks
½ cup all-purpose flour	¾ cup heavy cream
2½ cups hot chicken stock, fresh or canned	1 teaspoon salt
	¼ teaspoon white pepper
	1 teaspoon lemon juice

VELOUTÉ SAUCE: In a heavy 2- to 3-quart saucepan, melt the 6 table-spoons of butter, then stir in ½ cup of flour and cook, stirring constantly, over low heat for about a minute. Remove from heat, let cool a moment, and vigorously beat in the hot chicken stock. When the *roux* and liquid are blended, return to moderately high heat, stirring thoroughly until the sauce comes to a boil. Boil, stirring, for 1 minute, then remove from heat. With a clean whisk, blend the egg yolks and ¾ cup of cream together in a bowl. Whisk in the hot sauce, 2 tablespoons at a time, until ½ cup has been added. Still off the heat, reverse the process and slowly pour the egg yolk-cream mixture back into the remaining hot sauce, whisking until it is smooth and creamy. Bring to a boil over moderate heat, still stirring, and boil slowly for 10 seconds. Remove from the heat at once and season with salt, pepper and lemon juice. This makes about 3½ cups of very thick sauce.

THE FILLING AND TOPPING	
1 cup sautéed and diced chicken livers (about ½ pound), or 1 cup cooked and diced shrimp (about 1 pound raw shrimp in the shell), or ¼ cup finely chopped defrosted frozen artichoke hearts sautéed in 2 tablespoons butter with ¼ cup diced smoked or boiled ham	1 teaspoon finely chopped fresh parsley or tarragon
	Lemon juice
	Salt
	White pepper
	1 cup grated, imported Swiss cheese or Swiss and Parmesan combined
	4 tablespoons butter, in tiny pieces
	¼ to ½ cup heavy cream

THE FILLING AND TOPPING: Preheat the oven to 375°. In a large mix-ing bowl, combine the chicken livers, shrimp or sautéed ham and arti-choke hearts with 1 teaspoon parsley. (Sauté the artichoke hearts in 2 table-spoons of butter for 1 or 2 minutes, then add the ham and cook them for another minute or so.) Stir in the *duxelles* and ½ cup of *velouté* sauce. The mixture should be just thick enough to hold its shape in a spoon; add up to

Continued on next page 11

½ cup more of *velouté* sauce if necessary. Taste and season with lemon juice, salt and pepper. Spoon a scant 2 tablespoons of filling on the lower third of each *crêpe* and roll it up; do not tuck in the ends. Thin the remaining *velouté* sauce with cream until it flows heavily off a spoon. Butter a baking-serving dish large enough to hold all the rolled *crêpes* and spread a film of *velouté* sauce on the bottom. Arrange the *crêpes* side by side in the dish. Mask them with the rest of the sauce and sprinkle the cheese on top. Dot with bits of butter. Bake in the upper third of the oven for 15 to 20 minutes or until the sauce bubbles. The top should be lightly browned; if it isn't, slide the dish under a hot broiler for a few seconds. Serve at once.

Saucisson Chaud à la Lyonnaise
SAUSAGE WITH FRENCH POTATO SALAD

Serves 4 to 6

1 pound uncooked plain or garlic pork sausage, fresh or smoked (French, Italian or Polish)	¼ cup wine vinegar (preferably white)
	2 teaspoons salt
	½ teaspoon dry mustard
3 pounds firm boiling potatoes, sliced ¼-inch thick	½ to ¾ cup olive oil
Boiling salted water	2 tablespoons thinly sliced scallions including some green tops
¼ cup chicken stock, fresh or canned	4 tablespoons finely chopped fresh parsley

Following the directions in the recipe for *saucisson en croûte (page 2),* prick the sausage and simmer it uncovered in a deep skillet over moderate heat for 45 minutes.

While the sausage is simmering, cook the potato slices in a 3- to 4-quart saucepan in boiling salted water to cover for 12 to 15 minutes, or until they are done but not at all overcooked. Drain them thoroughly in a sieve or colander and transfer them to a large mixing or serving bowl. Heat the chicken stock and pour it over the warm potatoes, tossing them very gently once or twice, and let stand for several minutes until the stock is completely absorbed. In a small mixing bowl, stir the vinegar, salt and dry mustard together, add to the potatoes and toss very gently again. Let the potatoes stand for a few minutes to absorb the seasoning, then pour in the olive oil and sprinkle in the scallions and parsley. Turn the potatoes gently to coat them with the oil and herbs.

When the sausage has simmered for 45 minutes, lift it out of the skillet with tongs and drain it on paper towels. As soon as it is cool enough to handle, skin it and cut it into ½-inch slices. Serve the warm potato salad from a bowl or platter with the sausage slices arranged around it.

Sauce Mayonnaise

To make about 2 cups

3 egg yolks, at room temperature
1 to 3 teaspoons lemon juice or wine
    vinegar
1/2 teaspoon dry mustard

1/2 teaspoon salt
1/8 teaspoon white pepper
1 1/2 cups olive oil or vegetable oil or
    a combination of both
2 tablespoons boiling water (optional)

Warm a large mixing bowl in hot water, dry it quickly but thoroughly, and drop the egg yolks into it. With a wire whisk, rotary or electric beater, beat the yolks vigorously for about 2 minutes or until they thicken and cling to the whisk or beater. Add a teaspoon of the lemon juice or vinegar and the dry mustard, salt and pepper. Then beat in the oil, 1/2 teaspoon at a time; make sure each addition is absorbed before adding more. By the time 1/2 cup of oil has been beaten in, the sauce should be like thick cream. Add the rest of the oil by teaspoonfuls, beating constantly. Taste and season with lemon juice, salt and pepper if necessary. To make the mayonnaise creamier and lessen the danger of separating, beat in boiling water 1 tablespoon at a time. Keep the mayonnaise in the refrigerator, tightly covered, until ready to use. For *mayonnaise aux fines herbes*, add 2 tablespoons finely chopped parsley and 1 tablespoon each of finely cut fresh chives and fresh tarragon.

Sauce Hollandaise

To make about 1 1/2 cups

12 tablespoons butter (1 1/2
    quarter-pound sticks)
3 egg yolks

1 tablespoon lemon juice
1 tablespoon chilled butter
1 tablespoon heavy cream
Salt
White pepper

In a small, heavy pan over low heat, melt 12 tablespoons of butter without letting it brown. Set the butter aside and keep it warm. Off the heat, in a 1 1/2- to 2-quart enameled or stainless-steel saucepan, beat the egg yolks vigorously with a wire whisk for 1 minute or until they become thick; the bottom of the pan should show through when the whisk is drawn across it. Beat in the lemon juice. Then place the pan over very low heat and stir in the 1 tablespoon of chilled butter with the whisk. Stir constantly, lifting the pan off the stove occasionally to prevent it from overheating, until the butter has been absorbed and the mixture thickens enough to coat the wires of the whisk lightly. Remove the pan from the heat and beat in the cream. Still off the heat, pour in the warm, melted butter by droplets, stirring constantly with the whisk. The sauce will thicken into a heavy cream. Taste the hollandaise and season with salt and white pepper.

Sauce Béarnaise
HOLLANDAISE WITH TARRAGON AND WHITE WINE

To make about 1½ to 2 cups

¼ cup tarragon wine vinegar
¼ cup dry white wine
1 tablespoon finely chopped shallots
   or scallions
2 tablespoons finely cut fresh tarragon

or 2 teaspoons dried tarragon and
1 tablespoon finely chopped fresh
parsley
1½ cups *sauce hollandaise* (recipe
   page 13) made without lemon juice
Salt
White pepper

In a small saucepan, briskly boil the vinegar, wine, shallots and 1 table-spoon fresh or 2 teaspoons dried tarragon until reduced to 2 tablespoons. Strain the liquid through a fine sieve into a small mixing bowl, pressing down hard on the herbs with a spoon before discarding them. Then whisk the strained liquid into the *sauce hollandaise* along with 1 table-spoon of fresh tarragon or parsley. Taste and season with salt and pepper.

Terrine Maison
HOME-STYLE PÂTÉ

To serve 10 to 12

1 pound fresh pork fat, ground
1½ pounds lean pork, ground
1½ pounds calf's, beef or pork liver,
   ground
½ pound lean veal, ground
5 tablespoons butter
⅓ cup finely chopped shallots or
   scallions
½ teaspoon finely chopped garlic
½ pound whole chicken livers
¼ cup Cognac
3 tablespoons heavy cream

2 teaspoons lemon juice
2 tablespoons flour
1 egg, lightly beaten
½ teaspoon spice Parisienne or
   allspice
1½ tablespoons salt
Freshly ground black pepper
¼ pound cooked smoked beef tongue
   or baked ham cut in ¼- inch cubes
   (about 1 cup) (optional)
½ pound fresh pork fat back, the fat
   from a pork loin or fat salt pork,
   sliced into ⅛-inch strips or sheets
1 large bay leaf

Combine the ground meats in a large mixing bowl. In a heavy 8- to 10-inch skillet, melt 3 tablespoons of butter over moderate heat. When the foam subsides, stir in the shallots and garlic and cook, stirring frequently, for 5 minutes, or until soft but not brown. With a spatula, scrape into the bowl of meat.

   In the same skillet, melt 2 tablespoons of butter and cook the chicken livers for 3 or 4 minutes or until they have stiffened but are still pink inside. Remove the livers with a slotted spoon and set them aside on a plate. Pour the Cognac into the hot skillet and boil it, stirring and scraping in any browned bits that cling to the bottom or sides of the pan, until it has reduced to about 2 tablespoons. Pour this glaze over the meat and shallots. Set the skillet aside.

Add the cream, lemon juice, flour, egg, spice Parisienne or allspice, salt and a generous grinding of pepper to the meat mixture. Knead vigorously with both hands, then beat with a wooden spoon (or in an electric beater with a pastry arm) until all the ingredients are well blended and the mixture is smooth and fluffy. Lightly fold in the tongue or ham cubes if they are used. Because the mixture contains raw pork, sauté a spoonful of it in the waiting skillet before tasting it for seasoning. Add more seasoning then if needed.

Preheat the oven to 350° and line a deep, rectangular 2-quart mold which has a cover (a *terrine*, or a metal or glass baking pan) with thin strips or sheets of pork fat. Depending on their length, the strips may be arranged lengthwise or crosswise, but they should overlap slightly and completely cover the bottom and sides of the mold. If they are long enough, let them hang over the sides and later lap them back over the top of the filling; otherwise, save enough strips of the fat to cover the top of the *terrine*.

Spoon half of the meat mixture into the lined mold, pressing it down firmly and smoothing it with the back of the spoon or a rubber spatula. Cut the chicken livers into quarters or eighths, depending on their size, and lay them in a row down the center of the mold. Fill the mold with the remaining meat mixture.

Smooth the top with a spoon or spatula and bring the long strips of fat from the sides up over the meat or arrange additional strips over it. Lay a bay leaf on the fat, enclose the top of the mold snugly with foil, then cover tightly.

Place the mold in a large baking pan on the middle shelf of the oven. Pour in enough boiling water to reach at least halfway up the side of the mold and bake the *terrine* for 2 hours or until the fat and juices which will have risen to the top are clear yellow.

Remove the *terrine* from the oven and lift off the cover and aluminum foil. Loosely cover the mold with fresh foil and weight the *terrine* by placing a heavy pan, casserole or cutting board, weighing at least several pounds, on top of it. Let cool to room temperature, then refrigerate the *terrine*, with the weight still in place, until it is thoroughly chilled. To serve, remove the weight and the foil, and cut slices directly from the mold in which the *terrine* baked.

Sauce Vinaigrette
FRENCH OIL AND VINEGAR DRESSING

To make ½ cup

2 tablespoons white or red wine
    vinegar

Salt
Freshly ground black pepper
¼ teaspoon dry mustard (optional)
6 to 8 tablespoons olive oil

With a whisk or fork, beat the vinegar, a little salt and pepper and the mustard (if used) until the salt dissolves. Dribble in the oil a few drops at a time, beating constantly, until it is absorbed. Taste and season.

NOTE: Lemon juice may be substituted for the vinegar, or the sauce may be made with half lemon juice, half vinegar.

Omelette
FRENCH OMELET

To serve 1 to 2

3 eggs
Salt

Freshly ground black pepper
1 tablespoon butter
½ teaspoon soft butter

Break the eggs into a small mixing bowl, season with salt and pepper, and stir briskly with a table fork 20 to 30 seconds or until the whites and yolks are blended together. Heat an ungreased 7- to 8-inch omelet pan until it is very hot, drop in the tablespoon of butter and swirl it in the pan so that it melts quickly and coats the bottom and sides. When the foam begins to subside but before the butter browns, pour in the eggs.

Working quickly, stir the eggs with the flat of the fork, at the same time shaking the pan back and forth vigorously to prevent the eggs from sticking. In a few seconds, the eggs will form a film on the bottom of the pan and the top will thicken to a light, curded custard. Still shaking the pan with one hand, gently stir through the top custard with the other hand to spread the still-liquid eggs into the firmer areas; try not to pierce the bottom film. Then lift the edge closest to you with the fork and roll the omelet up lightly over to the far side of the pan. Let it rest for a moment on the lip of the pan, then tilt the pan and roll the omelet out onto a heated plate. Brush the top with soft butter and serve at once.

NOTE: To make a filled omelet, sprinkle a few tablespoons of grated cheese, finely chopped herbs or sautéed mushrooms over the eggs before rolling the omelet up. Do not stir in the filling. To serve more than 1 or 2, make several individual omelets. Large omelets are rarely successful.

Soups

Potage Queue de Boeuf
OXTAIL SOUP

To serve 4

3 tablespoons butter
1 tablespoon vegetable oil
2 pounds oxtail, cut in 1-inch
    sections
1 onion, thinly sliced
1 carrot, thinly sliced
2 tablespoons flour
2 quarts beef stock, fresh or canned

Bouquet garni made of 2 parsley
    sprigs, 2 celery stalks and 1 leek,
    tied together
1 teaspoon dried thyme
4 or 5 peppercorns
Salt
Freshly ground black pepper
½ cup finely diced carrots
½ cup finely diced turnips
1 to 2 tablespoons dry Madeira or port

In a heavy 4- to 6-quart saucepan or soup pot, melt 1 tablespoon of the butter with the oil over moderate heat. Add the oxtail and cook, turning frequently, until the pieces are golden brown on all sides. Using kitchen tongs, transfer the oxtail to a plate. Cook the sliced onion and carrot in the fat remaining in the pan for 8 to 10 minutes, or until they are soft and lightly browned. Stir in the flour and cook, stirring constantly, until the flour has browned. Remove the pan from the heat and let it cool slightly. Gradually beat in the beef stock, whisking vigorously. Bring to a boil and cook, stirring, until the soup is smooth and has begun to thicken. Return the oxtail to the pan together with the *bouquet garni,* thyme and peppercorns, and bring to a boil over high heat. Skim the fat from the surface, reduce the heat and simmer the soup, partially covered, for 3½ hours, skimming frequently. Lift out the oxtail with a slotted spoon and strain the soup through a fine sieve into a large mixing bowl. Let it settle for a few minutes, then skim off the surface fat. Taste the strained soup, season it with salt and pepper, and return it to the pan. Melt 2 tablespoons of butter in a 6- to 8-inch skillet and in it cook the diced carrots and turnips, stirring frequently, for 1 or 2 minutes or until they are coated with butter. Add the diced carrots and turnips and the oxtail to the soup and simmer the soup for 30 minutes, skimming the fat from the surface as necessary. To serve, ladle the soup into a tureen and stir in the wine.

Fonds de Cuisine
HOMEMADE BEEF AND CHICKEN STOCKS

To make 3 to 4 quarts

2 pounds beef shank and 4 pounds
    beef bones or 6 pounds chicken
    backs and necks
4 to 5 quarts cold water
2 onions, peeled

2 carrots, peeled
2 celery stalks with leaves, cut up
Bouquet garni, made of 6 parsley
    sprigs, 1 bay leaf, 2 garlic cloves
    and ½ teaspoon dried thyme,
    wrapped together in cheesecloth
1 tablespoon salt

Good soups depend on good stocks—and so do stews, casseroles, braised meats and vegetables, and many sauces. Here are recipes for three stocks (or *fonds de cuisine*) that are basic to French cooking.

SIMPLE STOCK: Place the beef and bones, or the chicken backs and necks in a soup pot or kettle, and add enough cold water to cover them by 1 inch. Bring to a boil over high heat, skimming off the scum that rises to the surface. Add the vegetables, *bouquet garni* and salt. Bring to a simmer, skimming if necessary, then partially cover and cook very slowly for 4 hours. Remove the bones and strain the stock through a fine sieve into a large bowl, pressing down hard on the vegetables and herbs before discarding them. Taste and season. Skim any fat from the surface or refrigerate until the fat solidifies on the top and can be removed. The stock will keep refrigerated for 3 or 4 days or can be frozen for future use. For richer taste boil down the strained and degreased stock until its flavor has concentrated.

BROWN BEEF STOCK: Preheat the oven to 450°. Roast the beef bones, onions and carrots in a shallow pan for 30 to 40 minutes, turning them occasionally. Transfer the bones and vegetables to a soup pot. Then discard the fat from the roasting pan, add 2 cups of water and bring to a boil over high heat, scraping in any browned bits clinging to the pan. Pour this into the soup pot and add the celery, *bouquet garni*, salt and cold water to cover. Proceed with the stock, following the directions above.

BROWN POULTRY STOCK: Over high heat, brown the chicken backs and necks in 2 tablespoons of vegetable oil in a large skillet. Transfer them to the soup pot and deglaze the skillet with a little water. Add this to the soup pot with the onions, carrots, celery, *bouquet garni*, salt and cold water to cover. Proceed with the stock, following the directions for simple stock.

Soupe au Pistou
VEGETABLE SOUP WITH GARLIC, BASIL AND TOMATO SAUCE

To serve 10 to 12

3 cups water
¾ cup dry white beans (Great
    Northern, marrow or navy)
4 tablespoons olive oil
1 cup diced onions
1 pound tomatoes, peeled, seeded and
    coarsely chopped (about 1½ cups)
3 quarts water
1½ cups diced carrots

1½ cups diced boiling potatoes
1 cup coarsely chopped leeks
    (optional)
½ cup coarsely chopped celery leaves
1 tablespoon salt
Freshly ground black pepper
1½ cups sliced fresh green string beans
1½ cups diced, unpeeled zucchini
½ cup broken pieces of spaghettini
2 pinches crumbled saffron threads

Bring 3 cups of water to a boil in a 2- to 3-quart saucepan. Drop in the dry beans and boil them for 2 minutes. Remove from the heat and let the beans soak for 1 hour. Return the pan to low heat and simmer uncovered for 1 to 1½ hours, or until the beans are tender. Drain the beans and reserve the cooking liquid. In a heavy soup pot or kettle, heat 4 tablespoons of olive oil. Stir in the diced onions and cook over moderate heat until limp and golden, then add the tomatoes and cook for 3 or 4 minutes longer. Pour in 3 quarts of water and bring to a boil over high heat. Add the carrots, potatoes, leeks, celery leaves, salt and a few grindings of pepper; reduce the heat and simmer uncovered for 15 minutes. Stir in the white beans, their cooking liquid, the green beans, zucchini, spaghettini and saffron, and simmer for 15 minutes, or until the vegetables are tender. Taste and season.

PISTOU

5 garlic cloves, finely chopped
½ cup finely cut fresh basil or
    5 tablespoons dried basil
2 tablespoons tomato paste
½ cup freshly grated Parmesan cheese

6 tablespoons olive oil
1 small slice stale French bread,
    finely crumbled (optional)
1½ cups freshly grated Parmesan
    cheese

Meanwhile, prepare the *pistou*. With a large mortar and pestle (or a wooden spoon and heavy bowl), mash the garlic and basil into a paste. Work in the tomato paste and ½ cup of the cheese, then beat in 6 tablespoons of olive oil, 1 tablespoon at a time. To serve, ladle the soup into a tureen. Thin the *pistou* with ½ cup of soup stock and stir as much of the *pistou* as you like into the soup. Sprinkle in the crumbled bread (optional). Pass the rest of the grated cheese separately.

Potage Purée de Pois Cassés

SPLIT PEA SOUP

To serve 4 to 6

2 cups dry green split peas
5 cups water or fresh or canned
   chicken stock
Bouquet garni, made of 2 parsley
   sprigs, 2 chopped celery tops and 1
   bay leaf, tied together
¼ teaspoon dried thyme
Ham bone (optional)
2 tablespoons butter
¼ pound salt pork, finely diced
½ cup finely chopped carrots
½ cup finely chopped onions

1 large leek, chopped (white part
   plus 2 inches of green) or 1 extra
   onion, finely chopped
1 cup coarsely chopped spinach or
   lettuce leaves
½ cup shelled fresh green peas (about
   ½ pound, unshelled) or substitute
   defrosted frozen peas
Salt
Freshly ground black pepper
½ pound baked ham, cut in ½-inch
   cubes (about 2 cups)
2 tablespoons soft butter

Wash the split peas thoroughly under cold running water. In a heavy 4- to 5-quart saucepan or a soup kettle, bring 5 cups of water or chicken stock to a boil and drop in the peas. Add the *bouquet garni,* the thyme and the ham bone, if you use it. Reduce the heat and simmer half covered for 30 minutes to 1 hour, or until the peas are tender but not mushy.

While the peas are simmering, melt 2 tablespoons of butter in a heavy 8- to 10-inch skillet, and in it brown the diced salt pork until it is crisp and renders its fat; remove the pork and discard it. In the fat remaining in the skillet, cook the carrots, onions, leek and spinach or lettuce leaves uncovered over moderate heat for 5 minutes, or until the onions are soft and the leaves have wilted. When the split peas are tender, add all of the vegetables including the fresh green peas to the soup and simmer uncovered for another 30 minutes. Remove and discard the *bouquet garni* and the ham bone, if used. Purée the soup through a food mill into a large bowl, and then rub it through a fine sieve back into the saucepan. Taste and season with salt and freshly ground black pepper, add the ham cubes and bring the soup to a simmer over low heat. If the soup seems too thick, thin it with a little chicken stock or water.

Before serving, remove the pan from the heat and stir the soft butter into the soup, 1 tablespoon at a time. Ladle the soup into a large tureen or individual soup bowls.

Soupe à l'Oignon
FRENCH ONION SOUP

To serve 6 to 8

4 tablespoons butter
2 tablespoons vegetable oil
2 pounds onions, thinly sliced
   (about 7 cups)

1 teaspoon salt
3 tablespoons flour
2 quarts beef stock, fresh or canned,
   or beef and chicken stock combined

In a heavy 4- to 5-quart saucepan or a soup kettle, melt the butter with the oil over moderate heat. Stir in the onions and 1 teaspoon salt, and cook uncovered over low heat, stirring occasionally, for 20 to 30 minutes, or until the onions are a rich golden brown. Sprinkle flour over the onions and cook, stirring, for 2 or 3 minutes. Remove the pan from the heat. In a separate saucepan, bring the stock to a simmer, then stir the hot stock into the onions. Return the soup to low heat and simmer, partially covered, for another 30 or 40 minutes, occasionally skimming off the fat. Taste for seasoning, and add salt and pepper if needed.

CROÛTES
12 to 16 one-inch-thick slices of
   French bread
2 teaspoons olive oil

1 garlic clove, cut
1 cup grated, imported Swiss cheese
   or Swiss and freshly grated
   Parmesan cheese combined

While the soup simmers, make the *croûtes*. Preheat the oven to 325°. Spread the slices of bread in one layer on a baking sheet and bake for 15 minutes. With a pastry brush, lightly coat both sides of each slice with olive oil. Then turn the slices over and bake for another 15 minutes, or until the bread is completely dry and lightly browned. Rub each slice with the cut garlic clove and set aside.

To serve, place the *croûtes* in a large tureen or individual soup bowls and ladle the soup over them. Pass the grated cheese separately.

ALTERNATIVE: To make onion soup *gratinée*, preheat the oven to 375°. Ladle the soup into an ovenproof tureen or individual soup bowls, top with *croûtes*, and spread the grated cheese on top. Sprinkle the cheese with a little melted butter or olive oil. Bake for 10 to 20 minutes, or until the cheese has melted, then slide the soup under a hot broiler for a minute or two to brown the top if desired.

Potage Parmentier; Vichyssoise

LEEK OR ONION AND POTATO SOUP

To serve 6 to 8

4 cups peeled and coarsely chopped
    potatoes
3 cups thinly sliced leeks (white part
    plus 2 inches of green) or substitute
    3 cups thinly sliced onions
2 quarts chicken stock, fresh or

canned, or substitute water or a
    combination of chicken stock and
    water
1 teaspoon salt
Freshly ground black pepper
½ cup heavy cream
3 tablespoons finely cut fresh chives
    or finely chopped fresh parsley

In a heavy 6-quart saucepan or a soup kettle, simmer the potatoes, leeks, chicken stock and salt partially covered for 40 to 50 minutes or until the vegetables are tender. Force the soup through a food mill or sieve into a mixing bowl and then pour back into the pan. Season the soup with salt and a few grindings of pepper, and stir in the cream. Before serving, return the soup to low heat and bring it to a simmer. Ladle the soup into a tureen or individual soup bowls. Serve garnished with fresh chives or fresh parsley.

VICHYSSOISE: When Louis Diat was chef at the Ritz-Carlton Hotel in New York City half a century ago, he devised vichyssoise—a cold version of *potage Parmentier*. To make it, force the soup through a food mill or sieve, then through a fine sieve back into the pan. Season and stir in 1½ cups of heavy cream. (Do not use a blender; the mixture will be too smooth.) Chill the soup until it is very cold. Serve it garnished with finely cut fresh chives.

Bouillabaisse

MEDITERRANEAN FISHERMAN'S SOUP WITH HOT PEPPER SAUCE

To serve 8 to 10

COURT BOUILLON
2 cups thinly sliced onions
1 cup thinly sliced leeks
¾ cup olive oil
8 cups water or 2 cups dry white wine
    and 6 cups water
2 pounds fish heads, bones and
    trimmings
3 pounds ripe tomatoes, coarsely

chopped (about 6 cups)
½ cup fresh fennel or ½ teaspoon dried
    fennel seeds, crushed
1 teaspoon finely chopped garlic
1 three-inch strip fresh orange peel
1 teaspoon dried thyme
2 parsley sprigs
1 bay leaf
¼ teaspoon crushed saffron threads
Salt
Freshly ground black pepper

In a heavy 4- to 6-quart saucepan, cook the onions and leeks in the oil over low heat, stirring frequently, for 5 minutes, or until they are tender but not brown (additional onions may be substituted for the leeks). Add the water or wine and water, the fish trimmings, tomatoes, herbs and seasonings, and cook uncovered over moderate heat for 30 minutes.

ROUILLE

2 small green peppers, seeded and
  cut in small squares
1 dry chili pepper or a few drops of
  Tabasco added to the finished sauce
1 cup water

2 canned pimientos, drained and dried
4 garlic cloves, coarsely chopped
6 tablespoons olive oil
1 to 3 tablespoons fine dry bread
  crumbs

THE ROUILLE: Meanwhile, prepare the *rouille*. In a 1½- to 2-quart sauce-pan, simmer the green peppers and chili pepper in 1 cup of water for 10 minutes, or until they are tender. Drain them thoroughly and dry them with paper towels. Then, with a large mortar and pestle, or a mixing bowl and wooden spoon, mash the peppers, pimiento and garlic to a smooth paste. Slowly beat in the olive oil and add enough bread crumbs to make the sauce thick enough to hold its shape in a spoon. Taste and season with Tabasco if you have omitted the chili pepper.

A quicker but less authentic way to make *rouille* is to combine the simmered peppers, the pimiento, garlic and the olive oil in an electric blender. Blend at low speed until they are smooth, adding more oil if the blender clogs. With a rubber spatula, transfer the sauce to a bowl and stir in enough bread crumbs to make it thick enough to hold its shape in a spoon. Taste and season with Tabasco if you have omitted the chili pepper. Set aside.

FISH AND SEAFOOD

2 two-pound live lobsters, cut up and
  cracked (see directions in recipe for
  homard à l'américaine, page 39)
1½ pounds each of three kinds of
  firm, white fish cut into 2-inch
  serving pieces: halibut, red
  snapper, bass, haddock, pollack,

hake, cod, yellow pike, lake trout,
  whitefish, rockfish
1 eel, cut in 2-inch pieces (optional)
2 pounds live mussels (optional)
2 pounds fresh or frozen sea scallops,
  cut in halves or quarters (optional)
12 *croûtes* (see *soupe à l'oignon*,
  page 21)

ASSEMBLING THE SOUP: When the court bouillon is done, strain it through a large fine sieve into a soup pot or kettle, pressing down hard on the fish trimmings and vegetables with the back of a spoon to extract their juices before discarding them. Bring the strained stock to a boil over high heat and add the lobster. Boil briskly for 5 minutes, then add the fish (and the eel, if you wish) and cook another 5 minutes. Finally, add the mussels and scallops (optional) and boil 5 minutes longer. Taste for seasoning.

To serve, remove the fish and seafood from the soup with a slotted spoon and arrange them on a heated platter. Ladle the soup into a large tureen. Thin the *rouille* with 2 or 3 tablespoons of soup and pour it into a sauce-boat. At the table, place a *croûte* in each individual soup bowl, ladle in the soup over it, and arrange fish and seafood on top. Pass the *rouille* separately.

Potage Crème d'Asperges

CREAM OF ASPARAGUS SOUP

To serve 4 to 6

2 pounds fresh asparagus
6 cups chicken stock, fresh or canned
1 teaspoon salt
7 tablespoons butter
6 tablespoons flour

2 tablespoons finely chopped shallots
  or scallions
2 egg yolks
¾ cup heavy cream
2 tablespoons soft butter
Salt
White pepper

With a small sharp knife (*not* a vegetable peeler), peel each asparagus stalk of its skin and tough outer flesh. At the butt end the peeling may be as thick as ¹⁄₁₆ inch, but it should gradually become paper thin as the knife cuts and slides toward the tip. Cut off the tips where the scales end and trim away any oversized scales. Trim off and discard about ¼ inch from the butt ends and cut the rest of the stalks into ½-inch lengths; set aside. In a 3- to 4-quart saucepan, bring the chicken stock and the salt to a boil over moderate heat. Drop in the asparagus tips and boil slowly for 5 to 8 minutes, or until they are just tender. Drain the stock into a bowl and set the tips aside in another.

In the same saucepan, melt 5 tablespoons of the butter over moderate heat. Stir in the 6 tablespoons of flour, then cook over low heat, stirring constantly, for 1 or 2 minutes. Do not let this *roux* brown. Remove the pan from the heat, let it cool for a few seconds, then pour in the stock, beating constantly with a wire whisk to blend the stock and the *roux*. Return the pan to moderate heat and stir until this cream soup base comes to a boil, thickens and is perfectly smooth. Turn the heat down and let the soup base simmer very gently.

Melt the remaining 2 tablespoons of butter in an 8- to 10-inch enameled or stainless-steel skillet. When the foam subsides, stir in the cut-up asparagus stalks and the shallots, and toss them in the butter over moderate heat for 3 minutes. Stir the stalks and shallots into the simmering soup base and cook over low heat, stirring occasionally, for 15 minutes or until the asparagus is tender.

Purée the soup through a food mill into a mixing bowl and then again through a fine sieve back into the pan. With a wire whisk, blend the egg yolks and cream together in a medium-sized mixing bowl. Whisk in the puréed soup, 2 tablespoons at a time, until ½ cup has been added. Then reverse the process and slowly whisk the now-warmed egg-yolk-and-cream mixture into the soup. Bring to a boil, and boil for 30 seconds, stirring constantly. Remove the pan from the heat and stir in the 2 tablespoons of soft butter, 1 tablespoon at a time. Taste the soup and season it with salt and white pepper. Add the reserved asparagus tips and ladle the soup into a tureen or into individual soup bowls.

Garbure
MAIN-COURSE MEAT AND CABBAGE SOUP

To serve 10 to 12

Water
¾ cup dry white beans (Great Northern, marrow or navy)
2 pounds lean salt pork in 1 piece
1 ham bone (optional)
3 pounds cabbage, shredded (about 12 cups)
4 medium-sized white turnips, cut in small chunks
2 carrots, sliced
3 onions, thickly sliced
2 leeks, white part plus 2 inches of green, thickly sliced (optional)
4 garlic cloves, crushed
Bouquet garni made of 8 parsley sprigs, 3 celery tops and 1 bay leaf tied together
½ teaspoon dried thyme, crumbled
1 pound uncooked garlic pork sausage, fresh or smoked (French, Italian or Polish)
6 firm boiling potatoes, cut in chunks
Salt
Freshly ground black pepper
Croûtes (page 21)

Bring 3 cups of water to a bubbling boil in a heavy 6- to 8-quart soup pot or kettle. Drop the beans in and boil them briskly for 2 minutes. Remove the pot from the heat and let the beans soak for 1 hour. While the beans are soaking, blanch and partially cook the salt pork by simmering it in 1 quart of water for 1 hour; drain on paper towels and pat dry.

When the beans have soaked, drain off the water and measure it. Add more water, enough to make 3½ quarts, and return to the soup pot. Add the blanched salt pork, the ham bone (optional), the cabbage, turnips, carrots, onions, leeks (optional), garlic, *bouquet garni* and thyme, and bring to a boil over high heat. Reduce the heat and simmer, partially covered, for 45 minutes. Then add the sausage (pricked in 4 or 5 places with the tip of a knife) and the potatoes, and simmer for another 45 minutes, or until the vegetables are tender. Discard the ham bone and *bouquet garni*. Remove and slice the salt pork and sausage. Taste the soup and season it with salt and pepper. Then ladle it into a large tureen or individual soup bowls, over the *croûtes*. Serve the meat separately on a heated platter.

Potage Crème de Champignons

CREAM OF MUSHROOM SOUP

To serve 4 to 6

1½ pounds fresh mushrooms	6 cups chicken stock, fresh or canned
9 tablespoons butter (1 quarter-pound stick plus 1 tablespoon)	2 egg yolks
	¾ cup heavy cream
2 finely chopped shallots or scallions	Salt
6 tablespoons flour	White pepper

Separate the mushroom caps and stems. Then slice half the mushroom caps about ⅛ inch thick and coarsely chop the remaining caps and all the stems. In an 8- to 10-inch enameled or stainless-steel skillet (iron or aluminum will discolor the mushrooms), melt 2 tablespoons of the butter over moderate heat.

When the foam subsides, add the sliced mushrooms and cook them, tossing them constantly with a wooden spoon, for 2 minutes or until they are lightly colored. With a slotted spoon, transfer them to a bowl and set them aside. Melt an additional 2 tablespoons of butter in the same skillet and cook the chopped mushroom caps and stems and the shallots for 2 minutes. Set them aside in the skillet.

In a heavy 4- to 6-quart saucepan, melt the remaining 5 tablespoons of butter over moderate heat. Remove the pan from the heat and stir in the 6 tablespoons of flour, then cook over low heat, stirring constantly, for 1 or 2 minutes. Do not let this *roux* brown. Remove the pan from the heat, let cool a few seconds, then pour in the chicken stock, beating constantly with a wire whisk to blend stock and *roux*. Return to heat and stir until this cream soup base comes to a boil, thickens and is perfectly smooth. Then add the chopped mushrooms and shallots and simmer, stirring occasionally, for 15 minutes.

Purée the soup through a food mill into a mixing bowl and then again through a fine sieve back into the saucepan. With a wire whisk, blend the egg yolks and the cream together in a bowl. Whisk in the hot puréed soup, 2 tablespoons at a time, until ½ cup has been added. Then reverse the process and slowly whisk the now-warm egg-yolk-and-cream mixture into the soup.

Bring to a boil, and boil for 30 seconds, stirring constantly. Remove the pan from the heat. Taste and season with salt and white pepper. Add the reserved sliced mushrooms and serve the soup from a tureen or individual soup bowls.

Potage Purée Soissonnaise
WHITE BEAN SOUP

To serve 6 to 8

2 to 3 quarts chicken stock, fresh or canned

3 cups dry white beans (Great Northern, marrow or navy)

1 tablespoon butter

1 onion, finely chopped

1 carrot, finely chopped

2 leeks (the white part plus 2 inches of the green), finely chopped, or 1 extra onion, finely chopped

2 cups water

¼ pound lean salt pork in one piece or 1 ham bone

Bouquet garni of 4 parsley sprigs, 2 celery tops and 1 bay leaf, tied together

Salt

Freshly ground black pepper

2 tablespoons soft butter

2 tablespoons finely chopped fresh parsley

In a heavy 4- to 6-quart saucepan or soup kettle, bring 2 quarts of chicken stock to a bubbling boil. Add the beans and boil uncovered for 2 minutes. Remove the pan from the heat and let the beans soak for 1 hour. Meanwhile, melt 1 tablespoon of butter in a heavy 6- to 8-inch skillet. When the foam subsides, stir in the onion, carrot and leeks, and cook, stirring frequently, for 5 minutes, or until they are barely tender. Set the vegetables aside in the skillet. Blanch the salt pork, if you are using it, in 2 cups of water in a small saucepan by simmering it uncovered for 10 minutes. Set the pork aside on paper towels to drain.

Drain the soaked beans and measure the stock. Return the beans and stock to the saucepan together with enough additional stock or water to make 2 quarts. Add the vegetables, the blanched pork or ham bone, and the *bouquet garni* and bring to a boil over high heat. Reduce the heat and simmer the soup slowly, uncovered, for 2 hours, or until the beans are very tender. Discard the *bouquet garni* and the pork or ham bone. Drain the beans, saving all the stock, and rub them through a sieve or food mill into a bowl. Return the puréed beans to the pan and add enough of the stock to make the soup as thick as heavy cream. If it is too thick, use more chicken stock to thin it. Taste and season the soup with salt and pepper. Bring the soup to a simmer over moderate heat and cook, stirring frequently, until it is hot. Remove the pan from the heat and, off the heat, swirl in the 2 tablespoons of soft butter. To serve, ladle the soup into a large tureen or individual soup bowls and garnish with parsley.

Bourride

PROVENÇAL FISH SOUP WITH GARLIC MAYONNAISE

To serve 8 to 10

COURT BOUILLON

2 pounds fish heads, bones and
    trimmings
6 cups water
1 cup dry white wine
2 onions, thinly sliced
2 leeks, white part only, thinly sliced
    (optional)
2 tablespoons wine vinegar,
    preferably white
2 three-inch strips fresh orange peel
2 bay leaves
1 teaspoon fennel seeds
2 teaspoons salt

AÏOLI

1 tablespoon fine, dry bread crumbs

1 tablespoon wine vinegar
6 garlic cloves, coarsely chopped
7 egg yolks
½ teaspoon salt
⅛ teaspoon white pepper
1½ cups olive oil
1 tablespoon lemon juice

FISH

2 pounds each of three kinds of firm,
    white fish fillets or steaks such as
    haddock, porgy, cod, sole, perch,
    rockfish, pollack or halibut, cut in
    2-inch serving pieces

CROÛTES

12 croûtes (see recipe for soupe à
    l'oignon, page 21)

In a 4- to 6-quart saucepan, bring the court bouillon ingredients to a boil, partially cover the pan, and cook over low heat for 30 minutes. Meanwhile, make the aïoli. Soak the bread crumbs in 1 tablespoon of wine vinegar for 5 minutes, then squeeze the crumbs dry in the corner of a towel. With a large mortar and pestle or a small, heavy mixing bowl and wooden spoon, vigorously mash the crumbs and garlic to a smooth paste. Beat in 3 egg yolks, one at a time and, along with the third yolk, add the salt and pepper. When the mixture is thick and sticky, begin to beat in the olive oil a few drops at a time. As soon as the mixture resembles thick cream, transfer it to a large mixing bowl. With a wire whisk, rotary or electric beater, beat in the rest of the oil, 1 teaspoon at a time. The sauce will be like a thick mayonnaise. Season it with lemon juice, salt and pepper if needed. Spoon ⅔ cup of aïoli into a small sauceboat and cover with plastic wrap. Put the rest of the sauce (about 1⅓ cups) into a 3- to 4-quart saucepan.

Strain the court bouillon through a sieve into a bowl, pressing down hard on the vegetables and trimmings with a spoon before discarding them. Wash the pan and return the court bouillon to it. Add the fish, bring to a boil and simmer uncovered for 3 to 8 minutes, or until the fish is just firm to the touch. Watch the fish carefully; different kinds and thicknesses cook at different speeds. With a slotted spatula or spoon, transfer the pieces to a heated platter as soon as they are done. Cover the platter loosely to keep the fish warm.

Off the heat, beat the 4 remaining egg yolks, one at a time, into the *aïoli* in the saucepan. Add 1 cup of hot fish broth, beating constantly, then gradually beat in the remaining broth. Cook over low heat, stirring, until the soup is thick enough to coat the whisk lightly. Do not let it come to a boil. Season with salt, pepper, and lemon juice if needed.

To serve, pour the soup into a large tureen and bring it to the table with the platter of fish, the sauceboat of *aïoli*, and the *croûtes*. Place a *croûte* in the bottom of each individual soup bowl, lay one or several pieces of fish on top of the *croûte*, and ladle in the soup. Top with a dab of *aïoli* and pass the remaining sauce separately.

Potage Crécy

PURÉE OF CARROT SOUP

To serve 4 to 6

	2 tablespoons plain white raw rice
2 tablespoons butter	Salt
¾ cup finely chopped onions	White pepper
3 cups finely chopped carrots	½ cup heavy cream
1 quart chicken stock, fresh or canned	1 tablespoon soft butter
2 teaspoons tomato paste	8 to 12 carrot curls (optional)

In a heavy 3- to 4-quart saucepan, melt the butter over moderate heat. Stir in the onions and cook, stirring occasionally, for 5 minutes, or until they are soft but not browned. Add the carrots, chicken stock, tomato paste and rice, and simmer gently, uncovered, for 30 minutes. Purée the soup through a food mill into a clean saucepan. Season it with salt and white pepper, and stir in the cream.

Before serving, return the soup to low heat and bring it to a simmer. Remove the pan from the heat and stir in the tablespoon of soft butter. Ladle the soup into a tureen or into individual soup bowls and garnish with carrot curls if desired.

Fish

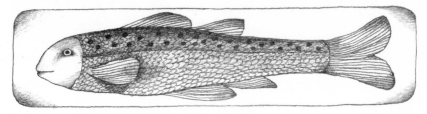

Bar Poché au Beurre Blanc

POACHED BASS WITH WHITE BUTTER SAUCE

To serve 6

COURT BOUILLON
2 quarts water
2 cups dry white wine
¼ cup wine vinegar
3 onions, thickly sliced
2 carrots, cut in 1-inch chunks
4 celery stalks with leaves, cut in

1-inch chunks
4 parsley sprigs
2 bay leaves
1 teaspoon finely cut fresh tarragon
   or ½ teaspoon dried tarragon
1 teaspoon finely cut fresh thyme or
   ½ teaspoon dried thyme
2 tablespoons salt
10 peppercorns

In a 6- to 8-quart enameled or stainless-steel pot or soup kettle, bring all the ingredients for the court bouillon to a boil over high heat. Partially cover the pot, reduce the heat and simmer for 30 minutes. Strain through a large, fine sieve into a fish poacher or a large, deep roasting pan which has a cover, and set aside to cool.

FISH
A 3- to 3½-pound whole striped bass,
   cleaned and scaled, but with head
   and tail left on (or substitute such

firm, white-meat fish as red snapper,
   haddock, cod, pollack, rockfish,
   whitefish or lake trout)
Fresh parsley sprigs

When the court bouillon is lukewarm, wash the fish inside and out under cold running water. Without drying it, wrap the fish in a long, double-thick piece of damp, washed cheesecloth, leaving at least 6 inches of cloth at each end to serve as handles for lifting the fish in and out of the pan. Twist the ends of the cloth and tie them with string, then place the fish on the rack of the poacher or roasting pan and lower the rack into the court bouillon. (If you are using a roasting pan, tie the ends of the cheesecloth to the handles of the pan.) The court bouillon should cover the fish by 1½ to 2 inches; add water if necessary.

Cover, and bring to a slow simmer over moderate heat; immediately reduce the heat and cook barely at a simmer for 15 minutes. Remove the pan from the heat and leave the fish in it for another 15 minutes. Then, using the ends of cheesecloth as handles, lift the fish from the pan and lay it on a large cutting board or platter. Open the cheesecloth and skin the fish with a small, sharp knife by making a cut in the skin at the base of the tail and gently pulling off the skin in strips from tail to gill. Holding both ends of the cheesecloth, carefully lift the fish and turn it over onto a heated serving platter. Peel off the skin on the upturned side. Garnish the fish with sprigs of fresh parsley and cover the platter loosely to keep the fish warm. (The court bouillon can be refrigerated or frozen and used again as fish stock.)

BEURRE BLANC
⅓ cup white-wine vinegar
⅓ cup dry white wine
2 tablespoons finely chopped shallots
   or scallions
½ teaspoon salt
⅛ teaspoon white pepper
½ pound butter, cut into 16
   tablespoon-sized pieces and
   thoroughly chilled

BEURRE BLANC: In a 1½- to 2-quart enameled saucepan, bring the vinegar, wine, shallots, salt and pepper to a boil over high heat and cook uncovered, stirring occasionally, until the liquid is reduced to about 1 tablespoon—it should be just a film on the bottom of the pan. Remove the pan from the heat and with a wire whisk immediately stir in 3 tablespoon-sized pieces of chilled butter, beating constantly until the butter is completely absorbed into the liquid.

Return the pan to the lowest possible heat and add the rest of the chilled butter 1 piece at a time, whisking constantly; and making sure that each piece is absorbed before adding the next. The finished sauce will be a thick, ivory-colored cream. Serve it at once in a warm, not hot, sauceboat.

To de-bone the fish for serving, divide the top layer into individual portions with a fish server without cutting through the spine. Leave the head and tail intact. Lift the portions with the fish server and a fork and arrange them attractively on another plate or platter. Then gently lift out the backbone in one piece, discard it and divide the bottom layer of fish into individual portions.

ALTERNATIVE: To serve poached bass cold, cook and skin it as described above. Cover the fish with plastic wrap or with aluminum foil and refrigerate it until it is thoroughly chilled. Serve the fish with *mayonnaise aux fines herbes (page 13)*, and garnish it with sprigs of fresh herbs, whole cherry tomatoes and lemon slices.

Coquilles Saint-Jacques à la Parisienne

SCALLOPS WITH MUSHROOMS IN WHITE WINE SAUCE

To serve 6

1½ cups thoroughly degreased
   fresh or canned chicken
   stock, or water
1½ cups dry white wine
3 sliced shallots or scallions
3 celery tops with leaves, cut in

2-inch pieces
4 parsley sprigs
1 bay leaf
10 whole peppercorns
2 pounds whole bay scallops, or sea
   scallops cut into ½-inch slices
¾ pound fresh mushrooms, sliced

Preheat the oven to 375°. In a heavy 3- to 4-quart saucepan, bring the stock, wine, shallots, celery, parsley, bay leaf and peppercorns to a boil over high heat. Reduce the heat, and simmer uncovered for 20 minutes. Strain this court bouillon through a sieve into a 10- to 12-inch enameled or stainless-steel skillet. Add the scallops and mushrooms, cover and simmer for 5 minutes. Transfer the scallops and mushrooms to a large mixing bowl. Quickly boil the remaining court bouillon down to 1 cup.

SAUCE PARISIENNE
4 tablespoons butter
5 tablespoons flour
¾ cup milk
2 egg yolks

¼ to ½ cup heavy cream
A few drops of lemon juice
1 teaspoon salt
White pepper
¼ cup grated imported Swiss cheese

SAUCE PARISIENNE: In a 2- to 3-quart enameled or stainless-steel saucepan, melt 4 tablespoons of butter over moderate heat. When the foam subsides, lift the pan from the heat and stir in the flour. Return to low heat and cook, stirring constantly, for a minute or two. Do not let this *roux* brown. Remove the pan from the heat and slowly pour in the reduced poaching liquid and the milk, whisking constantly. Then return to high heat and cook, stirring the sauce with a whisk. When it thickens and comes to a boil, reduce the heat and let it simmer slowly for 1 minute. Mix the egg yolks and ¼ cup cream together in a small bowl, and stir into it 2 tablespoons of the hot sauce. Add 2 more tablespoons of sauce, then whisk the now-heated egg-yolk-and-cream mixture back into the remaining sauce in the pan. Over moderate heat bring the sauce to a boil, stirring constantly, and boil for 30 seconds. Remove from heat and season with lemon juice, salt and pepper. The sauce should coat a spoon fairly thickly; if it is too thick, thin it with more cream.

With a bulb baster, draw up and discard any juices that may have accumulated under the scallops and mushrooms. Then pour in about ⅔ of the *sauce parisienne* and stir together gently. Butter 6 scallop shells set on a baking sheet or in a broiler pan, or 6 shallow 4-inch baking dishes, and spoon the scallop mixture into them. Mask with the remaining sauce and sprinkle with cheese. Bake the scallops in the top third of the oven for 10 to 15 minutes or until the sauce begins to bubble, then slide them under a hot broiler for 30 seconds to brown the tops if desired. Serve at once.

Coquilles Saint-Jacques à la Provençale
SCALLOPS SAUTÉED WITH GARLIC BUTTER SAUCE

To serve 4

	White pepper
2 pounds whole bay scallops, or sea	Flour
scallops cut into ¼-inch slices	2 tablespoons butter
Salt	3 tablespoons vegetable oil

Wash the scallops in cold water and dry them with paper towels. Season them with salt and pepper; then dip them in flour and shake them in a sieve or colander to remove all but a light dusting of flour. In a 10- to 12-inch enameled or stainless-steel skillet, melt 2 tablespoons of butter with the oil over moderate heat. When the foam subsides, sauté the scallops in two batches so they are not crowded in the pan, shaking the skillet and stirring the scallops until they are lightly browned. With a slotted spoon or spatula, transfer the scallops to a heated platter.

GARLIC BUTTER

8 tablespoons unsalted	2 tablespoons finely chopped fresh
butter (1 quarter-pound stick)	parsley
1 teaspoon finely chopped garlic	1 lemon, quartered

GARLIC BUTTER: In a 1½- to 2-quart saucepan, clarify 8 tablespoons of butter by melting it slowly, skimming off the foam. Spoon the clear butter on top into a 6- to 8-inch skillet and discard the milky solids at the bottom of the pan. Heat the butter until it sizzles, but do not let it brown. Remove it from the heat and quickly stir in the garlic. Pour the garlic butter over the scallops and serve at once, garnished with chopped parsley and lemon quarters.

Poisson Farci à la Florentine

BAKED FISH WITH SPINACH STUFFING

To serve 6 to 8

SPINACH STUFFING
4 tablespoons butter
3 tablespoons finely chopped shallots
  or scallions
½ cup finely chopped, cooked fresh
  spinach, squeezed dry and firmly
  packed (about ½ pound), or 1
  ten-ounce package frozen,

chopped spinach, defrosted and
  squeezed completely dry
2½ cups fresh white bread crumbs
  made in the blender from homemade-type bread (about 6 slices)
2 to 4 tablespoons heavy cream
¼ teaspoon lemon juice
½ teaspoon salt
Freshly ground black pepper

SPINACH STUFFING: Using a heavy 6- to 8-inch stainless-steel or enameled skillet, melt 4 tablespoons of butter over moderate heat and in it cook the shallots for 2 minutes, or until they are soft but not brown. Add the spinach and cook over high heat, stirring constantly, for 2 or 3 minutes to evaporate most of the moisture. Transfer to a large mixing bowl. Add the bread crumbs, cream, lemon juice, salt and a few grindings of pepper, and gently toss them all together. Season with more lemon juice, salt or pepper if needed.

FISH
A 4- to 5-pound whole red snapper,
  cleaned and scaled, with the
  backbone removed but the head
  and tail left on (or pollack, lake
  trout, cod, rockfish, whitefish,

salmon or mackerel)
6 tablespoons melted butter
1 cup dry white wine
1 tablespoon soft butter
Watercress sprigs, decoratively cut
  lemons

BAKING THE FISH: Preheat the oven to 400°. Wash the fish inside and out under running water, and dry it thoroughly with paper towels. Fill the fish with the stuffing, close the opening with small skewers, and crisscross kitchen string as you would lace a turkey. Brush 2 tablespoons of melted butter on the bottom of a shallow baking-and-serving dish large enough to hold the fish. (If you prefer to serve the fish from a platter, line the dish with a long piece of foil oiled or buttered on both sides to make it easy to handle later.) Place the fish in the dish, brush the top with another 2 tablespoons of melted butter, and salt and pepper it. Combine the rest of the melted butter with the wine and pour it around the fish. Bring to a simmer on top of the stove, then bake uncovered on the middle shelf of the oven, basting the fish every 5 to 7 minutes with the juices that will accumulate in the pan. If the wine evaporates, add up to ¾ cup more as needed.

In 40 to 50 minutes the fish should be just firm when pressed lightly with a finger. Remove the pan from the oven and, if the fish will be served from the baking dish, use a bulb baster to transfer the juices to a small pan. If the fish will be served from a platter, carefully lift the foil and fish from the baking dish, using the long ends of foil as handles. Gently slide the fish from the foil to the platter. Then pour the juices into a small pan.

Boil the juices down over high heat until they are syrupy. Remove from the heat, stir in 1 tablespoon of soft butter, and pour the sauce over the fish. Serve the fish alone or with *beurre blanc (page 30)* or hollandaise sauce *(page 13)*. Garnish it with watercress and decoratively cut lemons.

Darnes de Saumon Grillées au Beurre d'Escargots
BROILED SALMON STEAKS WITH GARLIC AND HERB BUTTER

To serve 4

GARLIC AND HERB BUTTER
8 tablespoons soft butter (1
   quarter-pound stick)
1 tablespoon finely chopped shallots
   or scallions

1 teaspoon finely chopped garlic
2 tablespoons finely chopped fresh
   parsley
Salt
Freshly ground black pepper

GARLIC AND HERB BUTTER: Cream the soft butter by beating it against the side of a small bowl with a wooden spoon until it is fluffy. Beat in the shallots, garlic, parsley, salt to taste and a few grindings of pepper.

FISH
4 salmon steaks, cut 1-inch thick and
   each weighing about ¾ pound
¼ cup butter, melted

Salt
Freshly ground black pepper
2 lemons, cut in quarters or slices

SALMON STEAKS: Preheat the broiler to very hot for 15 minutes. Dry the salmon thoroughly with paper towels. With a pastry brush, spread both sides of each steak with melted butter. Arrange the steaks on the rack of the broiling pan, and broil them with the top surface of the steaks 3 to 4 inches from the heat for 3 minutes on each side. Then baste them with any remaining melted butter or with the butter from the bottom of the broiling pan. Salt and pepper them and broil another 3 minutes. Then turn them over, baste again, and broil, basting once, for 5 to 8 minutes more, or until firm to the touch. With a spatula, transfer the steaks to a heated serving platter and garnish with lemon quarters or slices. Spread the garlic and herb butter over the steaks, or serve it separately in a sauceboat.

Filets de Soles à la Parisienne, Gratinés

FILLETS OF SOLE WITH WHITE WINE SAUCE

To serve 6 to 8

2 tablespoons finely chopped
   shallots or scallions
3 pounds gray, lemon, or petrale
   sole or flounder fillets, skinned and

cut into serving pieces all of the
   same size
Salt
Freshly ground black pepper
¾ cup dry white wine
Water

Preheat the oven to 350°. Butter the bottom of a shallow, flameproof baking-and-serving dish large enough to hold the fillets in one layer. Sprinkle the shallots over the bottom of the dish, lay the fillets over them, side by side, folding them in half if the fillets are less than ¼ inch thick. Season with salt and pepper. Pour in the wine and enough water to come almost to the top of the fish (about ½ to ¾ cup). Bring to a slow simmer on top of the stove, cover the dish with a sheet of buttered wax paper, and then poach on the middle shelf of the oven for 8 to 10 minutes, or until the fillets are just firm when pressed lightly with a finger. Remove the baking dish from the oven and set aside the wax paper. Increase the oven temperature to 425°. With a bulb baster, draw up all the liquid from the baking dish and strain into a 1½- to 2-quart enameled or stainless-steel saucepan. Re-cover the baking dish with the wax paper and set aside. Boil the poaching liquid over high heat until it has reduced to 1 cup.

SAUCE PARISIENNE
4 tablespoons butter
5 tablespoons flour
¾ cup milk
2 egg yolks
¼ to ½ cup heavy cream

A few drops of lemon juice
1 teaspoon salt
White pepper
2 to 3 tablespoons grated, imported
   Swiss cheese
2 teaspoons butter, cut in tiny pieces

SAUCE PARISIENNE: In a 2- to 3-quart enameled or stainless-steel saucepan, melt 4 tablespoons of butter over moderate heat. When the foam subsides, lift the pan from the heat and stir in the flour. Return to low heat and cook, stirring constantly, for a minute or two. Do not let this *roux* brown. Remove the pan from the heat and slowly pour in the reduced poaching liquid and the milk, whisking constantly. Then return to high heat and cook, stirring the sauce with a whisk. When it thickens and comes to a boil, reduce the heat and let it simmer slowly for 1 minute. Mix the egg yolks and ¼ cup cream together in a small bowl, and stir into it 2 tablespoons of the hot sauce. Add 2 more tablespoons of sauce, then whisk the now-heated egg-yolk-and-cream mixture back into the remaining sauce in the pan. Over moderate heat, bring the sauce to a boil, stirring constantly, and boil for 30 seconds. Remove it from the heat and season it with lemon juice, salt and a little white pepper. The sauce should be thick enough to coat the whisk lightly; if it is too thick, thin it with some or all of the remaining cream.

With a bulb baster, draw up any juices that have accumulated in the baking dish. Spread sauce under the fillets, lifting them gently with a spatula, then mask the tops of the fillets with the remaining sauce. Sprinkle on the grated cheese and dot the top with 2 teaspoons of butter. Bake in the top third of the oven for 10 to 15 minutes, or until the sauce bubbles, then slide the baking dish under the broiler for 30 seconds, or until it is lightly browned. Serve at once.

Truites à la Meunière
TROUT SAUTÉED IN BUTTER

To serve 4

	Salt
11 tablespoons butter (1 quarter-pound stick plus 3 tablespoons)	Flour
	1 tablespoon oil
4 whole fresh ½-pound trout or defrosted frozen trout, cleaned but with both the heads and tails left on	2 tablespoons lemon juice
	4 tablespoons finely chopped fresh parsley

In a 1½- to 2-quart saucepan, clarify 8 tablespoons of the butter by melting it slowly, skimming off the surface foam. Spoon the clear butter on top into a heavy 6- to 8-inch skillet and discard the milky solids at the bottom of the pan. Set aside.

Wash the trout under cold running water and dry them completely with paper towels. Season them inside and out with salt; dip them in flour and then shake them to remove all but a light dusting of the flour. In a heavy 10- to 12-inch skillet, melt the remaining 3 tablespoons of butter with the oil over moderately high heat. When the foam subsides, add the trout and sauté them over high heat, turning them with kitchen tongs, for 5 or 6 minutes on each side, or until they are a golden color and just firm when pressed lightly with a finger. Transfer them to a heated platter and cover lightly to keep warm. Cook the clarified butter over low heat until it browns lightly. Do not let it burn. Sprinkle the trout with lemon juice and parsley, pour the hot butter over them and serve immediately.

Filets de Soles Bonne Femme

FILLETS OF SOLE WITH MUSHROOM AND WINE SAUCE

To serve 6 to 8

3/4 pound fresh mushrooms
4 tablespoons butter
2 tablespoons vegetable oil
1 tablespoon finely chopped shallots
   or scallions
1 teaspoon lemon juice

3 pounds gray, lemon, or petrale sole
   or flounder fillets, skinned and cut
   into serving pieces all of the same
   size
Salt
Freshly ground black pepper
3/4 cup dry white wine
Water

Preheat the oven to 350°. Remove the caps from 12 to 16 of the mushrooms and slice all the stems and the rest of the caps. In a 6- to 8-inch enameled or stainless-steel skillet, melt 2 tablespoons of the butter with 1 tablespoon of the oil over moderate heat. Toss the whole mushroom caps in the hot fat for 1 or 2 minutes or until lightly browned, then set them aside in the skillet. In an 8- to 10-inch enameled or stainless-steel skillet, melt 2 tablespoons butter with 1 tablespoon oil over moderate heat. Add the sliced mushrooms and cook them, stirring constantly, for 2 minutes. Stir in the shallots, and cook for 1 minute. Then stir in the lemon juice.

Butter a shallow flameproof baking-and-serving dish large enough to hold the fillets in one layer. Lay the fillets in it side by side, folding them in half if they are less than 1/4 inch thick. Salt and pepper the fillets and spread with the mushroom-shallot mixture. Pour in the wine and enough water to come barely to the top of the fish. Bring to a slow simmer on top of the stove, cover with buttered wax paper, and then cook on the middle shelf of the oven for 8 to 10 minutes or until the fillets are just firm to the touch. Remove from the oven and discard the wax paper. With a bulb baster, draw up all the liquid from the dish and strain it into a 1½- to 2-quart saucepan. Set the baking dish aside, lightly covered to keep the fish warm. Boil the poaching liquid over high heat until it has reduced to 1 cup.

SAUCE CRÈME
4 tablespoons butter
4 tablespoons flour
2/3 to 3/4 cup heavy cream
1 tablespoon lemon juice

1 teaspoon salt
White pepper
4 to 8 tablespoons soft butter

SAUCE CRÈME: In a heavy 2- to 3-quart saucepan, melt 4 tablespoons of butter over moderate heat. When the foam subsides, remove from the heat and stir in the flour. Return to low heat and cook, stirring, for a minute or two. Remove from the heat and slowly add the reduced poaching liquid, whisking constantly. Return to high heat and cook, stirring with a whisk, until the sauce comes to a boil. It will be very thick. Whisk in ½ cup of cream and bring to a simmer again, stirring. Then thin it gradually with more cream added by spoonfuls until the sauce coats the spoon with a creamy layer. Season with lemon juice, salt and white pepper.

Just before serving, reheat the mushroom caps. Draw off with a bulb baster any juices that have accumulated in the baking dish. Remove the sauce from the heat and, by tablespoons, beat in as much of the soft butter as you wish. Spoon the sauce over the fish and arrange the mushroom caps on top. Serve at once.

Homard à l'Américaine
LOBSTER SIMMERED WITH WINE, TOMATOES AND HERBS

To serve 4 to 6

8 tablespoons butter (1 quarter-pound stick)
¼ cup finely chopped carrots
½ cup finely chopped onions
2 tablespoons finely chopped fresh parsley
1 teaspoon dried thyme
1 bay leaf
2 live lobsters, each 2 to 2½ pounds, cut into serving pieces
2 teaspoons salt
6 tablespoons olive or vegetable oil
⅓ cup Cognac

5 large tomatoes, peeled, seeded and coarsely chopped (about 3 cups)
¼ cup finely chopped shallots or scallions
1 cup dry white wine
1 cup chicken stock, fresh or canned
1 tablespoon tomato paste
1 teaspoon bottled meat extract
1 tablespoon flour
½ teaspoon lemon juice
1 tablespoon finely cut fresh tarragon or 1 teaspoon dried tarragon, crumbled
Salt
Freshly ground black pepper

In a heavy 3- to 4-quart flameproof casserole, melt 4 tablespoons of the butter over moderate heat. When the foam subsides, stir in the carrots and onions, and cook, stirring, for 5 to 8 minutes, or until they are soft but not brown. Remove from the heat, stir in 1 tablespoon of the parsley, the thyme and bay leaf.

Remove and discard the gelatinous sac near the head of each lobster, if the fish dealer did not. Scoop out the greenish-brown tomalley (or liver) and set aside. If there is black roe (or coral) save it. Sprinkle the lobster with 2 teaspoons salt. Then heat the oil almost to the smoking point in a heavy 10- to 12-inch skillet, and sauté the lobster over high heat, turning frequently, for 4 or 5 minutes, or until the shells are red.

Remove all but a film of oil from the skillet and, off the heat, flame the lobster with Cognac. Warm the Cognac in a small saucepan over low heat, ignite it with a match, and pour it flaming over the lobster a little at a

Continued on next page

time. Shake the skillet gently until the flame dies. Using tongs, transfer the lobster pieces to the casserole. Pour the juices from the skillet over them, and stir in the tomatoes and shallots.

In the same skillet, combine the wine, stock, tomato paste and meat extract. Bring this sauce to a boil, stirring constantly; boil for 2 minutes, then pour it over the lobster. Stir the contents of the casserole together until all the lobster pieces are coated with the sauce. Bring to a boil over high heat; immediately reduce the heat, cover the casserole tightly, and simmer for 30 minutes, basting 2 or 3 times with the juices.

Meanwhile cream the remaining 4 tablespoons of butter by beating it vigorously against the sides of a small bowl with a wooden spoon until it is fluffy. Beat in the coral, tomalley, flour, lemon juice, tarragon, 1 tablespoon of parsley and a little salt and pepper. Press through a sieve and set aside. When the lobster is done, arrange the pieces on a large, heated platter and cover loosely to keep the lobster warm, or set the platter in a 250° oven.

Strain the entire contents of the casserole through a fine sieve into a 2- to 3-quart saucepan, pressing down on the vegetables with a spoon before discarding them. Boil the juices over high heat until reduced by about ½. Turn the heat to low and beat in the creamed butter mixture, 1 tablespoon at a time. Cook the sauce over low heat for 5 minutes; do not let it boil. Taste for seasoning. To serve, pour the sauce over the lobster.

CUTTING THE LOBSTERS: If the fish dealer does not cut up the lobsters, make sure the claws are pegged and do the cutting yourself. Wash the lobsters in cold water and drain them. Then lay one lobster at a time on its underbelly on a chopping board and, with a towel wrapped around one hand for protection, grasp the lobster firmly. With a large, heavy, sharp knife, cut through the lobster behind the head; this severs the spinal cord and kills the lobster. Slice the tail into 4 or 5 crosswise pieces or cut it lengthwise in half. (This and all other cutting steps are easier if you put the knife into position and hit the back of it sharply with a hammer.) Then cut the claws from the lobster and separate the joints from the claws. Crack the flat side of each large claw. Remove the feelers, then cut the body section in half lengthwise. Don't forget to remove and discard the gelatinous sac near the head, but scoop out and save the tomalley— and the coral if there is any.

Poultry

Poule-au-pot

STUFFED CHICKEN SIMMERED WITH MEAT AND VEGETABLES

To serve 6

THE STUFFING

2 tablespoons butter
½ cup finely chopped onions
¾ cup plain white raw rice
1½ cups hot chicken stock, fresh or
   canned
½ pound fresh breakfast-type pork

sausage meat
2 chicken livers
4 tablespoons finely chopped fresh
   parsley
½ teaspoon dried thyme, crumbled
¼ cup heavy cream
Salt
Freshly ground black pepper

THE STUFFING: In a heavy 8- to 10-inch skillet, melt 2 tablespoons of butter over moderate heat. Add the chopped onions and cook, stirring frequently, for about 8 to 10 minutes, or until they are limp and lightly colored. Stir in the rice and cook, stirring, for 2 or 3 minutes without browning it. Pour 1½ cups of hot chicken stock over the onion-rice mixture, cover the skillet, reduce the heat, and simmer for 12 to 15 minutes, or until the rice is barely tender and the liquid absorbed. Transfer it to a bowl and set aside.

In the same skillet, fry the sausage meat over moderate heat, stirring with a fork to break it up, until it is lightly browned. Drain the sausage thoroughly and add it to the rice. Heat 2 tablespoons of the fat from the sausage in the skillet and quickly sauté the chicken livers until they stiffen and become lightly brown. Remove them from the pan and chop them coarsely; stir them into the rice and sausage mixture along with the parsley, thyme and cream. Season the finished stuffing with salt and a few grindings of pepper.

THE CHICKEN

A 5- to 6-pound stewing chicken   1 teaspoon salt

THE CHICKEN: Wash the chicken, neck, gizzard and heart under cold running water and dry thoroughly with paper towels. Rub the main cavity of the chicken with salt, and spoon in the stuffing loosely; don't overstuff it. Neatly sew up the openings and truss the chicken.

Continued on next page 41

THE STOCK

2 tablespoons butter
2 tablespoons vegetable oil
2 peeled onions, cut in half
3 celery stalks, cut in 2-inch chunks
1 veal knuckle, sawed in 2-inch pieces
1 leek, white part plus 2 inches of
green (optional)
4 parsley sprigs
1 bay leaf
2 quarts hot chicken stock, fresh or
canned
2 quarts water

THE STOCK: In a heavy 10- to 12-inch skillet, melt the 2 tablespoons of butter and oil over moderately high heat and in it brown the chicken lightly on all sides. Transfer the chicken to a heavy 6- to 8-quart soup pot or casserole and arrange the giblets, onion halves, celery chunks, veal knuckle, leek, parsley and bay leaf around it. Pour in the chicken stock and water. If the liquid doesn't rise at least 2 inches above the chicken, add more stock or water. Over high heat, bring the pot to a simmer, skimming the surface of scum as it appears. When the scum is gone, reduce the heat to low and partly cover the pot.

Simmer for 2½ hours, then remove the chicken to a plate; strain the stock through a fine sieve or double layer of cheesecloth into a large saucepan or bowl and skim off as much surface fat as possible. Discard the stewing vegetables. Return the chicken and stock to the pot, then proceed with the vegetable garnish below.

THE VEGETABLE GARNISH

6 peeled carrots, cut in 2-inch
   cylinders or olive shapes
4 peeled white turnips, quartered
3 peeled parsnips, quartered
6 medium leeks, white part plus 2
   inches of green, tied in a bunch
6 small potatoes, unpeeled if new

THE VEGETABLE GARNISH: Bring the chicken and stock to a simmer, add the carrots, turnips, parsnips and bunch of leeks, and cook slowly for about 30 minutes, or until the vegetables and chicken are tender. Meanwhile boil the potatoes in a small covered saucepan for 20 to 30 minutes; when they are done, drain them, cover and set aside.

To serve, transfer the bird to a carving board, cut off the trussing strings, and let it rest. With a slotted spoon, remove the vegetables from the stock to a heated platter and arrange them attractively with the potatoes. Carve the chicken in the kitchen and serve it arranged on a heated platter, surrounded with the stuffing. Serve the vegetables from their separate platter.

If you plan to serve the chicken without vegetables, let it simmer for 3 hours, or until tender. Remove the chicken to a carving board, cut off the trussing strings, and let it rest before carving.

NOTE: Save the stock for soup at a later meal, or cool and freeze it as a base for other soups and sauces.

Poulet Sauté à la Bordelaise
SAUTÉED CHICKEN WITH SHALLOTS AND ARTICHOKE HEARTS

To serve 4

A 2½- to 3-pound frying chicken,
  cut up
6 tablespoons butter
2 tablespoons vegetable oil
16 to 24 large whole peeled shallots,
  or 16 one-inch peeled white onions

Salt
Freshly ground black pepper
2 bay leaves
1 teaspoon lemon juice
1 nine-ounce package frozen
  artichoke hearts, defrosted and
  drained
½ cup chicken stock, fresh or canned

Wash the chicken quickly under cold running water and dry the pieces thoroughly with paper towels; if they are damp, they won't brown well. In a heavy 10- to 12-inch enameled or stainless-steel skillet or sauté pan, melt 4 tablespoons of the butter and the 2 tablespoons of oil over moderately high heat. When the foam begins to subside, brown the chicken a few pieces at a time, starting them skin side down and turning them with tongs. As the pieces become a rich golden brown, remove them to a plate.

When all the chicken is browned, add the shallots or onions to the skillet and cook them, shaking the pan to color them lightly and as evenly as possible. Pour off all but a thin film of fat and return the chicken to the skillet. Season with salt and pepper, lay the bay leaves on top and cover the pan. Cook over high heat until the fat splutters. At once reduce the heat and cook the chicken slowly, using a bulb baster or spoon to baste it with pan juices every 7 or 8 minutes.

Meanwhile, melt the remaining 2 tablespoons of butter in an 8- to 10-inch enameled or stainless-steel skillet. When the foam subsides, stir in the lemon juice. Add the artichoke hearts and toss them in the lemon butter until they glisten. Season them with salt, cover the skillet, and cook over low heat for 10 to 15 minutes or until the artichoke hearts are tender.

After the chicken has cooked for about 30 minutes it should be done, and its juices will run yellow when a thigh is pierced with the tip of a sharp knife. Remove the chicken from the skillet and arrange the pieces attractively on a large heated platter with the shallots or white onions and the artichoke hearts around them. Discard the bay leaves.

Pour the chicken stock into the juices remaining in the skillet and bring to a boil over high heat, scraping in any browned bits clinging to the bottom and sides of the pan. Boil for 2 or 3 minutes until the sauce is reduced to about ⅓ cup. Pour it over the chicken and serve at once.

ALTERNATIVE: If you like, you may cook the artichoke hearts with the chicken. In that case, omit the 2 tablespoons of butter and the lemon juice from the recipe. Add the artichoke hearts to the chicken after it has cooked with the shallots for 15 minutes and baste them well with the

Continued on next page 43

pan juices. Cover and cook, basting every 7 or 8 minutes, for 15 minutes longer, or until the chicken is done and the artichoke hearts are tender.

Poulet Sauté Vallée d'Auge
SAUTÉED CHICKEN WITH CALVADOS (OR APPLEJACK) AND CREAM SAUCE

To serve 4

A 2½- to 3-pound frying chicken, cut up
6 tablespoons butter
2 tablespoons vegetable oil
Salt
White pepper
⅓ cup Calvados or applejack
½ cup chicken stock, fresh or canned

2 tablespoons finely chopped shallots or scallions
¼ cup finely chopped celery
1 cup peeled, cored and coarsely chopped tart apples
½ teaspoon dried thyme, crumbled
2 egg yolks
½ cup heavy cream
Watercress or parsley sprigs

Following the directions in the recipe for *poulet sauté à la bordelaise (page 43)*, brown the chicken in 4 tablespoons of the butter and the oil in a heavy 8- to 10-inch skillet or sauté pan. Pour off all but a thin film of fat, return the browned chicken to the skillet and season it with salt and pepper. The next step is to flame the chicken—off the heat—with the Calvados or with applejack.

Experts pour the Calvados over the chicken and set it alight. A more reliable technique is to warm the Calvados first in a small saucepan over low heat, ignite it with a match and pour it flaming over the chicken a little at a time, shaking the skillet gently back and forth until the flame dies. Then pour in the stock and, with a wooden spoon, scrape in any browned bits clinging to the skillet. Set aside.

In a separate small saucepan or skillet, melt the remaining 2 tablespoons of butter over moderate heat and in it cook the shallots, celery, apples and thyme, stirring occasionally with a wooden spoon, for 10 minutes, or until they are soft but not brown. Spread them over the chicken, return it to high heat and bring the stock to a boil. Tightly cover the skillet, reduce the heat and simmer the chicken, basting it with pan juices every 7 or 8 minutes. After about 30 minutes, or when the chicken is tender, remove it from the skillet and arrange the pieces attractively on a large, heated ovenproof platter. Cover the chicken loosely with foil and keep it warm in a 250° oven while you make the sauce.

Strain the contents of the skillet through a fine sieve set over a small saucepan, pressing down hard on the vegetables and the apples with the back of a spoon to squeeze out all their juices. Let the sauce settle a minute, then skim off as much of the surface fat as possible. Boil the sauce over high heat, stirring occasionally, for 2 or 3 minutes, or until it is reduced to about ½ cup.

With a wire whisk, blend the egg yolks and cream in a bowl and gradually beat in all of the hot sauce, 1 tablespoon at a time. Pour back into the saucepan and cook over moderately low heat for 2 or 3 minutes, stirring constantly, until the sauce thickens to a heavy cream. Do not allow it to boil or it will curdle; if it seems to be getting too hot, lift the pan off the heat for a few seconds to cool it, stirring all the while. Taste and correct the seasoning with salt and white pepper. To serve, mask each piece of chicken with the sauce, and decorate the platter with bouquets of watercress or parsley sprigs.

Poulet Sauté à la Crème
SAUTÉED CHICKEN WITH CREAM SAUCE

To serve 4

A 2½- to 3-pound frying chicken,
  cut up
5 tablespoons butter
2 tablespoons vegetable oil
Salt

Freshly ground black pepper
1 cup sliced fresh mushrooms
¼ cup dry white wine
¾ cup heavy cream
2 tablespoons finely chopped fresh
  parsley

Following the directions in the recipe for *poulet sauté à la bordelaise (page 43)*, brown the chicken in 4 tablespoons of the butter and the oil in a heavy 8- to 10-inch skillet or sauté pan. Pour off all but a thin film of fat, return the chicken to the skillet and season it. Cover the skillet tightly and cook over high heat until the fat splutters. Immediately reduce the heat and cook the chicken slowly, basting it with pan juices every 7 or 8 minutes. After 30 minutes, or when the chicken is tender, remove it from the skillet and arrange the pieces attractively on a heated serving platter.

Add the mushrooms to the skillet and toss for 2 minutes, then pour in the wine and boil over high heat, stirring in any browned bits that cling to the pan. When the wine has almost cooked away, stir in the cream and cook it briskly for at least 3 or 4 minutes until it has reduced and thickened slightly. Taste and correct seasoning. Remove from heat and stir in the parsley, add the remaining 1 tablespoon of butter and tip the pan back and forth to blend it into the sauce. Pour the sauce and mushrooms over the chicken and serve at once.

Perdreaux Rôtis sur Canapés

ROAST PARTRIDGES ON LIVER CANAPÉS

To serve 6

½ pound butter

6 slices homemade-type white bread cut ¼ inch thick

¼ pound fresh pork fat, diced

2 tablespoons finely chopped shallots or scallions

6 partridge livers or 3 chicken livers

2 tablespoons dry Madeira

½ teaspoon dried tarragon, crumbled

1½ teaspoons salt

6 one-pound, oven-ready young

partridges, rock Cornish game hens, squab chickens, baby pheasants, or jumbo squabs

7 tablespoons soft butter

½ teaspoon dried tarragon, crumbled

3 tablespoons vegetable oil

12 four-inch strips fresh pork fat, sliced paper thin

6 tablespoons butter, melted

½ cup dry Madeira

1 cup beef stock, fresh or canned

1 teaspoon lemon juice

Clarify the ½ pound of butter (nearly 1 pound in all is needed for this recipe) in a small, heavy saucepan or skillet by melting it slowly, skimming off the surface foam. Spoon the clear butter on top into a bowl and discard the milky solids at the bottom of the pan. Trim the crusts off the bread to make uniformly sized squares or rectangles. In a heavy 10- to 12-inch skillet, heat the clarified butter, then sauté the bread, 2 or 3 slices at a time, until it is golden brown on both sides. Set the sautéed bread aside on a baking sheet.

In a heavy 10- to 12-inch skillet, cook the pork dice over moderate heat, stirring or shaking the pan frequently, until they are crisp and brown and have rendered all of their fat. With a slotted spoon, remove the pork dice and discard them. Cook the shallots in the fat remaining in the pan over moderate heat, stirring constantly, for 2 minutes or until they are soft but not brown. Add the livers and cook them, stirring or shaking the skillet constantly, for 2 or 3 minutes, or until the livers are lightly browned. Remove the livers and, with a rubber spatula, scrape the entire contents of the skillet into a small bowl. Chop the livers very fine, almost to a purée, and combine them with the shallots. Stir in the Madeira, tarragon and 1 teaspoon of salt, and beat the mixture with a wooden spoon until it is smooth and thoroughly blended. Spread each slice of sautéed bread with about 1 tablespoon of the liver mixture. Place on a baking sheet and set aside.

Preheat the oven to 500°. Wash the partridges quickly under running water and dry them thoroughly inside and out with paper towels. Cream 6 tablespoons of the soft butter by beating it vigorously against the sides of a small bowl with a wooden spoon until it is fluffy; beat in ½ teaspoon each of tarragon and salt. Spread 1 tablespoon of this seasoned butter inside each partridge. Neatly truss the partridges with white kitchen string. Brush each partridge generously with vegetable oil. Lay 2 strips of fresh pork fat side by side over the breast and thighs of each bird and tie in place—crisscrossing the string around the bird to hold the pork firmly.

Then lay the birds on their backs on a rack in a large, shallow roasting pan and bake them for 10 minutes. Reduce the heat to 425°, baste the partridges with the melted butter and turn them on their right side. In 5 minutes, turn the birds on their left side and baste again. Bake the partridges, basting and turning them every 5 minutes, for 20 to 30 minutes longer, or until the juices that run out of their vents when the birds are lifted are clear yellow with no trace of pink and the drumsticks feel soft to the touch. Transfer the birds to a heated platter, cut off all the strings, and discard the strips of pork. Cover the partridges loosely with aluminum foil to keep them warm.

Pour off all but 2 tablespoons of fat from the roasting pan, add ½ cup of Madeira and bring to a boil on top of the stove over high heat, stirring and scraping in with a wooden spoon any browned bits clinging to the pan. Boil briskly for 1 or 2 minutes, or until the Madeira has reduced to about ¼ cup, then stir in the beef stock and continue boiling and stirring until the sauce thickens and is reduced to about ¾ cup. Off the heat, swirl in the remaining 1 tablespoon of soft butter and the lemon juice.

To serve, put the canapés under a hot broiler for 30 seconds, or until they are bubbling hot. Arrange the canapés on a heated serving platter and place a partridge on each canapé. Spoon the sauce over the birds and serve at once.

Fricassée de Poulet à l'Ancienne

OLD-FASHIONED CHICKEN FRICASSEE

To serve 4

A 2½- to 3-pound frying chicken,
   cut up
8 tablespoons butter (1 quarter-pound
   stick)
Salt
White pepper
¼ cup flour
3 cups hot chicken stock, fresh or
   canned
Bouquet garni made of 4 parsley

sprigs and 1 bay leaf, tied together
¼ teaspoon dried thyme, crumbled
⅔ cup chicken stock, fresh or canned
16 to 24 peeled white onions, about
   1 inch in diameter
¾ pound fresh mushrooms, whole if
   small, sliced or quartered if large
1 teaspoon lemon juice
2 egg yolks
½ cup heavy cream
2 tablespoons finely chopped fresh
   parsley

Wash the chicken quickly under cold running water and dry the pieces thoroughly with paper towels. In a heavy 2- to 3-quart flameproof casserole, melt 6 tablespoons of the butter over moderate heat. Using tongs, lay a few

Continued on next page

pieces of chicken at a time in the butter and cook them, turning them once or twice, for about 5 minutes, or until they stiffen slightly and are no longer pink. Do not let them brown. Remove to a plate and season with salt and white pepper.

With a wooden spoon, stir the flour into the butter remaining in the casserole and cook over low heat, stirring constantly, for 1 or 2 minutes without letting it brown. Remove from heat. Slowly pour in the hot chicken stock, beating vigorously to blend *roux* and liquid. Return to heat, whisking constantly until the sauce thickens and comes to a boil. Then reduce the heat and let the sauce simmer slowly for 1 minute.

Return the chicken to the casserole together with the juices that have collected on the plate, and add the *bouquet garni* and thyme. The sauce should almost cover the chicken; add more stock if it doesn't. Bring to a boil, cover, reduce heat and simmer for 30 minutes.

Meanwhile, combine ⅔ cup stock, the remaining 2 tablespoons butter and the onions in an 8- to 10-inch enameled or stainless-steel skillet. Bring to a boil, cover, and simmer over low heat for 15 to 20 minutes, or until the onions are tender when pierced with the tip of a sharp knife. With a slotted spoon, transfer the onions to a bowl. Stir the mushrooms and lemon juice into the stock remaining in the skillet. Bring to a boil, cover and simmer for 5 minutes. Add the mushrooms to the onions. Boil the liquid remaining in the skillet until it has reduced to 2 or 3 tablespoons, and pour it into the simmering casserole of chicken.

To test the chicken for doneness, pierce a thigh with the tip of a sharp knife; the juices should run pale yellow. With tongs, transfer the chicken to a plate and discard the *bouquet garni*. Skim the fat from the surface of the sauce, which by now should be as thick as heavy cream; if it isn't, boil the sauce rapidly uncovered until it reaches the desired consistency. With a wire whisk, blend the egg yolks and cream together in a bowl. Whisk in the hot sauce, 2 tablespoons at a time, until ½ cup has been added; then reverse the process and whisk the egg-yolk-and-cream mixture back into the remaining hot sauce. Bring it to a boil, stirring constantly, then boil slowly for 30 seconds. Taste and correct the seasoning with salt, white pepper and a few drops of lemon juice. Strain through a fine sieve into a large bowl.

Wash the casserole, arrange the chicken pieces, onions and mushrooms attractively in it, and pour the sauce over them. Do not use any juices that have accumulated under the chicken unless the sauce needs thinning. Before serving, cover the casserole and simmer it over moderate heat for 5 to 10 minutes, or until the chicken is hot. Do not let the sauce come to a boil again. Serve the chicken from the casserole or arranged on a heated platter, masked with sauce and sprinkled with parsley.

Caneton aux Navets

DUCK WITH TURNIPS

To serve 4

A 5-pound duck
1 teaspoon salt
2 tablespoons vegetable oil
1 tablespoon butter
1 onion, thinly sliced
1 carrot, thinly sliced
Salt
Freshly ground black pepper
¼ teaspoon dried thyme, crumbled

Bouquet garni made of 4 parsley
  sprigs and 1 bay leaf, tied together
1½ pounds peeled white turnips, cut
  in quarters or 2-inch-long olive
  shapes
¾ cup boiling brown duck stock
  (recipe, page 50) or fresh or canned
  chicken stock
A few drops of lemon juice
1 tablespoon finely chopped fresh
  parsley

Preheat the oven to 325°. Wash the duck and giblets under cold running water and dry with paper towels. Set the giblets aside. Rub the cavity of the duck with 1 teaspoon salt, then truss the duck neatly. In a heavy 10- to 12-inch skillet, heat the oil almost to the smoking point and in it brown the duck on all sides, turning it with tongs or two spoons.

In a heavy enameled casserole, just large enough to hold the duck comfortably, melt 1 tablespoon butter over low heat. In it, cook the sliced onions and carrots over low heat, stirring occasionally for about 10 minutes, or until they are limp and lightly colored. Place the duck on top of them, season with salt and pepper, and add the thyme and *bouquet garni*. Cover the casserole, draping a piece of foil over the duck if the cover isn't snug, and braise it on the middle shelf of the oven for 1 hour.

Remove the duck from the casserole and strain the braising juices and vegetables through a fine sieve into a small mixing bowl, pressing down hard on the vegetables with a spoon to extract their juices before discarding them. Let the juices settle, then skim off as much surface fat as possible. Return the duck to the casserole and arrange the turnips around it. Pour in the strained juices and either boiling brown duck stock or chicken stock. The liquid should almost cover the turnips; if it doesn't, add more boiling stock. Bring to a simmer on top of the stove, cover the casserole and return it to the oven for 15 to 20 minutes or until the turnips are tender when they are pierced with the tip of a sharp knife.

Remove the casserole from the oven and increase the heat to 500°. Transfer the duck to a rack set in a shallow roasting pan and return it to the oven for 10 minutes to glaze to a deep brown. (Glazing isn't essential, but it improves the appearance of the duck and crisps the skin. This step can be omitted.) Cut off the trussing strings and place the duck on a heated platter. Arrange the turnips around the duck or at one end of the platter. Skim as much fat off the braising sauce as possible; taste and season with lemon

Continued on next page

juice, salt and pepper. Carve the duck in the kitchen or at the table and serve the braising sauce in a bowl, sprinkled with parsley.

BROWN DUCK STOCK	1 celery stalk, coarsely chopped
2 tablespoons vegetable oil	Duck neck, gizzard, heart and liver,
1 onion, coarsely chopped	cut up
1 carrot, coarsely chopped	2 cups chicken stock, fresh or canned

BROWN DUCK STOCK: While the duck is roasting, heat 2 tablespoons of oil in a heavy 2- or 3-quart saucepan. When the oil is very hot, brown the chopped onion, carrot and celery over moderate heat, stirring occasionally for about 10 minutes, or until they are lightly colored. Add the duck neck, gizzard, heart and liver and cook, stirring frequently, until they are deep brown. Pour in 2 cups of chicken stock, bring to a boil, reduce heat and simmer partly covered for 1 hour. Strain the stock through a fine sieve into a bowl, then skim off the surface fat. There should be at least ¾ cup of stock.

VARIATION I: WITH OLIVES. Simmer 2 dozen ripe green olives (often called California-style) uncovered in 1 quart of boiling water for 2 or 3 minutes. Drain. Braise them with the duck in place of the turnips.

VARIATION II: WITH PEAS. Simmer 1½ pounds of shelled fresh green peas uncovered in 1 quart of boiling salted water for 5 minutes. Drain the peas in a sieve or colander and plunge them into cold water to stop their cooking. Braise them with the duck in place of the turnips.

Poulet Rôti
ROAST CHICKEN

To serve 4

	3 tablespoons melted butter
A 3½- to 4-pound roasting chicken	1 tablespoon vegetable oil
2 tablespoons soft butter	1 onion, sliced
½ teaspoon lemon juice	1 carrot, cut in ½-inch chunks
Salt	1 celery stalk, cut in ½-inch chunks
Freshly ground black pepper	1 cup chicken stock, fresh or canned

Preheat the oven to 450°. Wash the chicken quickly under cold running water and dry it thoroughly inside and out with paper towels. Cream the soft butter, beating it vigorously against the side of a small bowl with a wooden spoon until it is fluffy. Beat in the lemon juice, ¼ teaspoon salt and a few grindings of pepper. Spread the seasoned butter inside the chicken. Neatly truss the chicken with white kitchen string. Combine the melted butter and oil and brush about half of it over the outside of the chicken.

Place the chicken on its side on a rack in a shallow roasting pan just large enough to hold it comfortably—about 9 by 12 inches—and place on the middle shelf of the oven. After 10 minutes, turn the chicken onto its other side. Brush with butter and oil and roast for another 10 minutes. Reduce the oven heat to 350°. Turn the chicken on its back, brush it with butter and oil and salt it lightly. Spread the vegetables in the bottom of the pan. Roast the chicken, basting it every 10 minutes with butter and oil while they last, then use a bulb baster or spoon to baste it with pan juices. After 60 minutes, test the chicken for doneness by lifting it with a wooden spoon inserted in the tail opening. When the juices that run out are yellow, it is done. If they are pink, cook a few minutes longer. Transfer the bird to a carving board, cut off the trussing strings, and let it rest for 5 minutes or so before serving.

Meanwhile, make the sauce. Stir the chicken stock into the roasting pan and bring to a boil over high heat, stirring and scraping in any browned bits clinging to the bottom and sides of the pan. Boil briskly for 2 or 3 minutes until the sauce has the desired intensity of flavor. Strain through a sieve, pressing down hard on the vegetables with the back of a spoon before discarding them. Skim off as much surface fat as possible, and taste for seasoning. The chicken may be carved in the kitchen or at the table. Serve the sauce separately.

Poulet en Cocotte Bonne Femme

CASSEROLE-ROASTED CHICKEN WITH VEGETABLES

To serve 4

	in diameter
A 3½- to 4-pound roasting chicken	6 peeled carrots, cut in 2-inch
4 tablespoons soft butter	cylinders or olive shapes
¼ teaspoon finely chopped garlic	16 one-inch potato balls, or potatoes
½ teaspoon dried thyme, crumbled	cut in 2-inch olive shapes
¼ pound salt pork, diced	Salt
2 cups water	Freshly ground black pepper
5 tablespoons butter	Bouquet garni made of 4 parsley
16 peeled white onions, about 1 inch	sprigs and 1 bay leaf, tied together

Preheat the oven to 350°. Wash the chicken quickly under cold running water and dry it thoroughly inside and out with paper towels. Cream 2 tablespoons of soft butter until it is fluffy, and beat in the garlic and thyme. Spread the seasoned butter inside the chicken. Truss the chicken and rub the outside with the remaining 2 tablespoons of soft butter.

Blanch the salt pork dice by simmering them in 2 cups of water for 5 minutes; drain on paper towels and pat dry. In a heavy, enameled oval

Continued on next page

casserole just large enough to hold the chicken comfortably, melt 1 table-spoon of the butter over moderate heat and in it brown the pork dice, stirring them or shaking the casserole frequently, until they are crisp and golden. Remove them with a slotted spoon and set aside to drain on paper towels. In the rendered fat left in the casserole, brown the chicken on all sides. Remove from heat and pour off all but a thin film of fat from the casserole. Return the chicken and the browned pork dice to it and set aside.

In a heavy 10- to 12-inch skillet, melt the remaining 4 tablespoons of butter over moderate heat and in it cook the onions, carrots, and potatoes, stirring frequently, for 5 minutes, or until coated with butter and lightly colored. Remove the vegetables and arrange around the chicken. Season with salt and pepper, add the *bouquet garni,* and cover the casserole. If the cover isn't snug, drape a piece of foil over the chicken before covering it.

On top of the stove, heat the casserole until the fat begins to splutter. Cook the chicken on the middle shelf of the oven, basting it every 20 minutes with the juices that will accumulate in the casserole. After 1¼ hours, start testing the chicken by lifting it with a wooden spoon inserted in its tail opening. When the juices that run out are yellow, it is done.

To serve, transfer the chicken to a heated platter and arrange the vegetables attractively around it. Discard the *bouquet garni* and skim as much surface fat as possible from the sauce left in the casserole. Taste the sauce and correct the seasoning. The chicken may be carved in the kitchen or at the table. Serve the sauce separately.

Coq au Vin à la Bourguignonne
CHICKEN SIMMERED IN RED WINE WITH ONIONS AND MUSHROOMS

To serve 4	in diameter
	2 cups water
THE ONIONS	1 tablespoon butter
½ pound lean salt pork, cut into	12 to 16 peeled white onions, about
lardons, 1¼-inch strips ¼ inch	1 inch in diameter

THE ONIONS *(oignons glacés à brun):* Preheat the oven to 350°. To remove excess saltiness, blanch the salt pork by simmering it in 2 cups of water for 5 minutes; drain on paper towels and pat dry. In a heavy 8- to 10-inch skillet, melt 1 tablespoon of butter over moderate heat, and in it brown the pork strips, stirring them or shaking the pan frequently, until they are crisp and golden. Remove them with a slotted spoon and set aside to drain on paper towels. Brown the onions in the rendered fat over moderately high heat, shaking the skillet occasionally to roll them around and color them as evenly as possible. Transfer the onions to a shallow baking dish large enough to hold them in one layer, and sprinkle them with a tablespoon or 2 of pork fat. Bake the onions uncovered, turning them once or twice, for 30 minutes, or until they are barely tender when pierced with the tip of a sharp knife. Remove from the oven, drain off fat, and set aside.

THE MUSHROOMS
2 tablespoons butter
2 tablespoons finely chopped shallots
or scallions
½ pound fresh mushrooms, whole if small, quartered or sliced if large

THE MUSHROOMS: Melt 2 tablespoons of butter over moderate heat in another 8- to 10-inch enameled or stainless-steel skillet. When the foam subsides, cook the shallots, stirring constantly with a wooden spoon, for 30 seconds. Add the mushrooms and cook them with the shallots, stirring and turning them frequently, for 2 or 3 minutes. Add to the onions and set aside.

THE CHICKEN
A 2½- to 3-pound frying chicken, cut up
¼ cup Cognac
Bouquet garni made of 4 parsley sprigs and 1 bay leaf, tied together
½ teaspoon dried thyme, crumbled
1 large garlic clove, finely chopped
2 cups red Burgundy or other dry red wine
2 tablespoons flour
½ cup beef or chicken stock, fresh or canned
2 tablespoons finely chopped fresh parsley

THE CHICKEN: Preheat the oven to 350°. Wash the chicken quickly under cold running water and dry the pieces thoroughly with paper towels. Re-heat the pork fat remaining in the first skillet, adding a few tablespoons of vegetable oil, if needed, to make a film of fat ⅛-inch deep. Brown the chicken, a few pieces at a time. Then pour off almost all of the fat from the skillet, add the Cognac and set it alight with a match; or warm the Cognac first in a small saucepan over low heat, ignite it with a match and pour it flaming over the chicken a little at a time, shaking the skillet back and forth until the flame dies. Transfer the chicken to a heavy 3- to 4-quart casserole, and add the browned pork, *bouquet garni*, thyme and garlic.

Boil the wine briskly in a 1- to 1½-quart enameled or stainless-steel saucepan to reduce it to 1½ cups. With a wooden spoon, stir the flour into the glaze remaining in the skillet in which the chicken browned, scraping in any browned bits clinging to the bottom and sides of the pan. Pour the reduced wine into the skillet and stir in the stock. Over high heat, bring this sauce to a boil, stirring constantly, and cook it until thick and smooth. Strain through a fine sieve over the chicken.

Bring the casserole to a boil over high heat, cover tightly, and place on the middle shelf of the oven. After 30 minutes, gently stir in the onions and mushrooms, and moisten them well with the sauce. Continue baking for an-other 10 to 15 minutes, or until the chicken is tender. Discard the *bouquet garni*. Taste and correct the seasoning of the sauce, then serve the chicken from the casserole, or arrange the pieces attractively on a deep heated platter, pour the sauce and vegetables over them and sprinkle with chopped parsley.

Meat

Boeuf Bourguignon

BEEF STEW WITH RED WINE

To serve 6 to 8

THE ONIONS

½ pound lean salt pork, cut into strips
   (*lardons*) about 1½ inches long
and ¼ inch in diameter
1 quart water
1 tablespoon butter
18 to 24 peeled white onions, about
   1 inch in diameter

To ensure that no one element in your *boeuf bourguignon* is overdone, cook the onions, mushrooms and beef separately before finally combining them. Although the different steps may be taken simultaneously, it is easier to deal with them one at a time.

THE ONIONS: Preheat the oven to 350°. To remove excess saltiness, the salt pork should be blanched by simmering it in 1 quart of water for 5 minutes; drain on paper towels and pat dry. In a heavy 8- to 10-inch skillet, melt 1 tablespoon of butter over moderate heat, and in it brown the pork, stirring the pieces frequently, until they are crisp and golden. Remove them with a slotted spoon and set aside to drain on paper towels. In the rendered fat left in the skillet, brown the onions lightly over moderately high heat, shaking the pan occasionally to roll them around and color them as evenly as possible. Transfer the onions to a shallow baking dish large enough to hold them in one layer, and sprinkle them with 3 tablespoons of pork fat. (Set the skillet aside, leaving the rest of the fat in it.) Bake the onions uncovered, turning them once or twice, for 30 minutes or until they are barely tender when pierced with the tip of a sharp knife. Remove from the oven and set aside.

THE MUSHROOMS
3 tablespoons butter
¾ pound fresh mushrooms, whole if
   small, quartered or sliced if large

THE MUSHROOMS: While the onions are baking or after they are done, melt 3 tablespoons of butter over moderate heat in an 8- to 10-inch enameled or stainless-steel skillet. When the foam subsides, cook the mushrooms, tossing and turning them frequently, for 2 or 3 minutes, or until they are slightly soft. Add the mushrooms to the onions and set aside.

3 pounds lean boneless beef chuck or rump, cut in 2-inch chunks	2 cups red Burgundy or other dry red wine
Bouquet garni made of 4 parsley sprigs and 1 bay leaf, tied together	1 tablespoon tomato paste
2 tablespoons finely chopped shallots or scallions	1 teaspoon finely chopped garlic
	1 teaspoon dried thyme
¼ cup very finely chopped carrots	1 teaspoon salt
3 tablespoons flour	Freshly ground black pepper
1 cup hot beef stock, fresh or canned	2 tablespoons finely chopped fresh parsley

THE BEEF: Make sure the oven is preheated to 350°. Pour almost all of the rendered pork fat from the skillet in which the onions browned into a small bowl, leaving just enough to make a thin film about ¹⁄₁₆ inch deep on the bottom of the pan. Over moderately high heat, bring the fat almost to the smoking point. Dry the beef with paper towels, then brown it in the fat, 4 or 5 chunks at a time to avoid crowding the skillet. Add more pork fat as needed. When the chunks are brown on all sides, remove them with kitchen tongs to a heavy, flameproof 4- to 6-quart casserole. Bury the *bouquet garni* in the meat.

After all the beef is browned, add the chopped shallots and carrots to the fat remaining in the pan and cook them over low heat, stirring frequently, until they are lightly colored. Stir in the flour. (If the mixture looks dry, add a little more pork fat.) Return the skillet to low heat and cook, stirring constantly, until the flour begins to brown lightly, but be careful it doesn't burn. Remove from the heat, let cool a moment, then pour in the hot beef stock, blending vigorously with a wire whisk. Blend in the wine and the tomato paste and bring to a boil, whisking constantly as the sauce thickens. Mix in the garlic, thyme, sautéed pork strips, salt and a few grindings of black pepper, and pour the sauce over the beef, stirring gently to moisten it thoroughly. The sauce should almost, but not quite, cover the meat; add more wine or beef stock if needed. Bring to a boil on top of the stove, cover tightly, and place the casserole in the lower third of the oven. Let the beef cook, regulating the oven heat so the meat simmers slowly, for 2 to 3 hours, or until the meat is tender when pierced with the tip of a sharp knife. Then gently stir the browned onions and mushrooms, together with any juices that may have accumulated under them, into the casserole. With a large spoon, gently mix the beef and vegetables with the sauce in the casserole. Continue baking for another 15 minutes. To serve, remove the *bouquet garni* and skim off any fat from the surface. Taste the sauce and season it with salt and pepper if needed. Sprinkle the beef with parsley and serve it directly from the casserole, or for more formal occasions, transfer it to a deep, heated platter.

Sauté de Lapin au Vin Blanc
RABBIT STEWED IN WHITE WINE SAUCE

To serve 4 to 6

A 2½- to 3-pound fresh rabbit or
  defrosted frozen rabbit, cut in
  serving pieces
1 cup dry white wine
2 tablespoons white wine vinegar
¼ cup olive oil
1 onion, thinly sliced
½ teaspoon dried thyme
1 bay leaf, crumbled
2 teaspoons finely chopped fresh
  parsley

½ teaspoon salt
Freshly ground black pepper
¼ pound lean salt pork, diced
2 cups water
1 tablespoon butter
12 to 16 peeled white onions, about
  1 inch in diameter
3 tablespoons finely chopped shallots
½ teaspoon finely chopped garlic
2 tablespoons flour
1½ cups beef stock, fresh or canned
Bouquet garni made of 4 parsley
  sprigs and 1 bay leaf, tied together

Wash the rabbit under running water and dry it with paper towels. Combine ½ cup of the wine, 1 tablespoon wine vinegar, olive oil, the sliced onion, thyme, bay leaf, parsley, salt and pepper for the marinade in a shallow baking dish or casserole. Marinate the rabbit 6 hours at room temperature, 12 to 24 hours refrigerated. Turn the pieces every few hours.

Simmer the pork dice in 2 cups of water for 5 minutes; drain and pat dry with paper towels. In a heavy 10- to 12-inch skillet, melt 1 tablespoon of butter over moderate heat and in it brown the pork dice until they are crisp and golden. Set the pork aside and pour most of the fat into a bowl, leaving just a film on the bottom of the skillet. Brown the onions in the fat left in the skillet, then transfer them to a bowl.

Remove the rabbit from the marinade and dry it with paper towels. Reserve the marinade. Brown the rabbit in the skillet, adding more fat as needed, then transfer the pieces to a heavy flameproof 2- to 3-quart casserole. Pour off almost all the fat from the skillet, add the shallots and garlic and cook, stirring constantly, for 2 minutes. Stir in the flour and cook, stirring over low heat 1 minute. Remove from heat and pour in the remaining ½ cup wine and stock, stirring constantly. Cook over moderate heat, stirring, until the sauce thickens. Then pour it over the rabbit and add the *bouquet garni,* reserved marinade and browned pork dice. Preheat the oven to 350°.

Bring the stew to a boil on top of the stove, cover, and cook on the middle shelf of the oven for 40 minutes. Gently stir in the onions and cook for another 20 minutes, or until the rabbit is tender when pierced with the tip of a sharp knife. Just before serving, stir the remaining 1 tablespoon of vinegar into the sauce and taste for seasoning. Serve the stew directly from the casserole.

Noisettes de Porc aux Pruneaux
LOIN FILLETS OF PORK WITH PRUNES AND CREAM SAUCE

To serve 4

2 dozen large dried prunes
1 cup dry white wine
6 *noisettes* of pork (fully trimmed and boned rib end of loin, tied and sliced 1½ inches thick)
Salt

Freshly ground black pepper
Flour
2 tablespoons butter
1 tablespoon vegetable oil
½ cup chicken stock, fresh or canned
½ cup heavy cream
2 teaspoons red currant jelly
A few drops of lemon juice

In a 2- to 3-quart enameled saucepan soak the prunes in wine at room temperature, turning them occasionally, for 4 hours or longer if possible. Then cook them over moderate heat for 10 minutes, or until the prunes are tender. Drain, and set the prunes and wine aside separately.

Season the *noisettes* with salt and pepper. Dip them in flour, then shake off all but a fine dusting of flour. In a heavy 10- to 12-inch skillet or sauté pan, melt the butter with the oil over moderate heat. When the foam subsides, brown the *noisettes* for about 3 minutes on each side or until they are a rich golden color. Transfer them with tongs from the skillet to a plate.

After the *noisettes* are browned, pour off almost all the fat from the skillet, leaving just enough to film the bottom. Add the wine in which the prunes cooked and boil it briskly, uncovered, until it almost cooks away. Pour in the chicken stock and bring to a boil again. Return the *noisettes* to the pan, cover and simmer gently over low heat for 30 to 40 minutes, or until the *noisettes* are tender when pierced with the tip of a sharp knife. With tongs, transfer the *noisettes* to a deep, heated platter, cut off the strings and cover them or set them in a 250° oven to keep warm.

Thoroughly degrease the stock remaining in the skillet, pour in the cream and bring it to a boil, stirring and scraping in any brown bits that cling to the skillet. Boil the sauce briskly, stirring constantly, until it is thick enough to coat the back of a spoon. Then stir in the prunes, jelly and lemon juice, and cook, stirring gently and constantly until the jelly is dissolved and the prunes heated through. Taste and correct seasoning. With a slotted spoon lift out the prunes and arrange them around the *noisettes*. Spoon the sauce over the *noisettes* and prunes and serve at once.

Boeuf à la Mode

POT ROAST OF BEEF BRAISED IN RED WINE

To serve 10 to 12

THE BEEF
1 tablespoon salt
1 teaspoon coarsely ground black
  pepper
A 5-pound boneless beef chuck or
  bottom round roast at least 5
  inches in diameter, trimmed and
  tied

THE MARINADE
3 cups red Burgundy or other dry red
  wine
1 cup thinly sliced onions
3/4 cup thinly sliced carrots
1 teaspoon finely chopped garlic
2 bay leaves, crumbled
2 tablespoons finely chopped fresh
  parsley
1 teaspoon dried thyme, crumbled

MARINATING THE BEEF: Press 1 tablespoon of salt and 1 teaspoon of pepper into the surface of the beef. In a large glass, porcelain or stainless-steel bowl, mix the marinade ingredients. Add the beef and turn it in the marinade until it is well moistened on all sides. Let it marinate for at least 6 hours at room temperature or 12 to 24 hours in the refrigerator, turning it over every few hours.

THE ONIONS AND CARROTS À BRUN
1/2 pound fresh pork fat, diced
20 to 24 white onions, about 1 inch

in diameter, peeled
6 to 8 carrots, peeled and cut into
  1 1/2-inch cylinders or olive shapes

THE ONIONS AND CARROTS À BRUN: Preheat the oven to 350 °. In a heavy 10- to 12-inch skillet, sauté the diced pork fat over moderate heat, stirring constantly, until crisp and brown. Remove the diced pork fat and reserve it. In the fat left in the skillet, brown the whole onions and the carrots lightly over moderately high heat, shaking the pan occasionally to roll them around and color them as evenly as possible. Transfer them to a shallow baking dish large enough to hold them in one layer, and sprinkle them with about 3 tablespoons of pork fat. (Set the skillet aside, without removing the remaining fat.) Bake the onions and carrots uncovered on the middle shelf of the oven, turning and basting them once or twice, for 30 minutes, or until they are barely tender. Remove from the oven, pour out the cooking fat and set the vegetables aside.

THE BRAISING STOCK
4 tablespoons butter
1/3 cup Cognac
2 calf's feet and / or 1 large veal
  knuckle, sawed into pieces
2 medium tomatoes, peeled, seeded
  and coarsely chopped

Bouquet garni made of 6 parsley
  sprigs, 1 bay leaf and the white
  part of 1 leek, tied together
3 cups beef stock, fresh or canned
Salt
Freshly ground black pepper
1/2 cup finely chopped fresh parsley

BRAISING THE BEEF: While the vegetables bake or when they are done, remove the beef from the marinade and dry it thoroughly with paper towels. Strain the marinade into a small bowl, and drain the vegetables on paper towels. Heat the pork fat remaining in the skillet to the smoking point and brown the beef over moderate heat until it is richly colored on all sides. While the beef is browning, melt 4 tablespoons of butter in a heavy, 6-quart flameproof casserole or Dutch oven. Add the marinated vegetables and cook over low heat, turning frequently, until most of their moisture has boiled away and they are lightly colored. When the beef is browned, use a bulb baster to draw off all but a thin film of fat from the skillet.

The next step is to flame the beef. Experts simply flame the beef with Cognac directly in the pan. But a more reliable way is to warm the Cognac first in a small saucepan over low heat, ignite it with a match, and pour it flaming over the beef a little at a time, shaking the skillet gently until the flame dies. Transfer the beef to the casserole and surround it with the pieces of calf's feet and / or veal knuckle, the chopped tomatoes, the diced pork fat and the *bouquet garni*.

Pour the strained marinade and 3 cups of beef stock into the skillet, and bring them to a boil over high heat, stirring and scraping in any browned bits that cling to the pan. Boil briskly for 1 or 2 minutes, then pour it into the casserole. The liquid should come about halfway up the side of the meat; add more beef stock if needed. Bring the casserole to a boil on top of the stove, then cover tightly and place on the middle shelf of the oven. Regulate oven heat so the beef simmers slowly, and turn and baste the meat 2 or 3 times during the cooking. After 2½ to 3 hours the meat should be tender when pierced with the tip of a sharp knife.

To serve the beef and the vegetables hot, transfer the beef from the casserole to a plate. Remove and discard the bones and *bouquet garni* and strain the rest of the contents of the casserole through a large, fine sieve into a 3- to 4-quart saucepan, pressing down hard on the vegetables before discarding them. Let the strained braising liquid, or sauce, settle for a few minutes, then skim as much fat as possible from the surface. Boil the sauce briskly over high heat until it has been reduced to half its original quantity (about 3 to 4 cups). Taste and season with salt and pepper. Return the meat and sauce to the casserole and add the baked onions and carrots. Simmer slowly on top of the stove to heat the beef and vegetables thoroughly. Transfer the beef to a carving board to remove the strings. Then arrange the roast on a large heated platter, surrounded with the onions and carrots. Spoon some of the sauce over it, and serve the rest separately in a warm sauceboat.

Continued on next page

2 to 4 cups beef stock, fresh or canned	½ teaspoon dried thyme, crumbled
	½ bay leaf
3 envelopes unflavored gelatin	10 peppercorns
3 egg whites	1 teaspoon salt
½ teaspoon lemon juice	½ cup dry Madeira

BOEUF À LA MODE EN GELÉE (cold pot roast of beef in aspic): To prepare the cold version of *boeuf à la mode*, let the beef cool for an hour in the braising liquid, turning it once or twice. Transfer the beef to a platter, let it cool to room temperature, then wrap and refrigerate it. Strain the braising liquid; cool, cover and refrigerate it. Cool, cover and refrigerate the baked onions and carrots.

When the braising liquid is thoroughly chilled, carefully remove and discard all of the fat that has solidified on the surface. In a 2- or 3-quart saucepan, melt the braising liquid over low heat and then measure it. Add enough beef stock to make 5 cups in all, and return it to the pan. Soften the gelatin in an additional 1 cup of cold fresh stock, and add it. Beat the egg whites to a froth with a wire whisk, and stir them into the stock, together with the lemon juice, thyme, bay leaf, peppercorns and salt. Bring to a boil over moderate heat, stirring constantly. When the aspic begins to froth and rise, remove the pan from the heat. Let it rest off the heat for 5 minutes, then strain it into a deep bowl through a fine sieve lined with a dampened kitchen towel. Allow the aspic to drain without disturbing it at any point. When it has drained completely through, add the Madeira, and taste and season the aspic with more salt if needed. Pour a thin layer of aspic—about ⅛ inch thick—into the bottom of a large serving platter, and refrigerate it until the aspic is set. Then carve the cold beef into ¼-inch slices and arrange the meat, onions and carrots attractively on the platter. Heat about ¾ cup of the aspic in a small pan just until it melts, then set it in a bowl filled with crushed ice or ice cubes immersed in water. Stir the aspic gently with a metal spoon until it thickens almost to the point of setting. Working quickly, spread a thin glaze of aspic over the sliced beef and vegetables. Chill until the aspic sets. Repeat this process two more times to make three coatings of aspic—melting and chilling for each layer. Refrigerate the platter until the glaze is firm. Meanwhile, melt the remaining aspic and pour it into a large flat roasting pan to make a sheet or film no more than ¼ inch deep; chill it.

When all the aspic is very firm, remove the roasting pan from the refrigerator, and score the sheet of aspic into diamonds with the tip of a sharp knife by cutting crossing diagonal lines about 1 to 1½ inches apart. Arrange the diamonds decoratively around the aspic-covered beef. Chop any scraps into fine dice, and garnish the platter with it as fancifully as you like. You can even put the chopped aspic into a pastry bag with a plain tip and press the aspic out in scrolls on the beef.

Cassoulet

CASSEROLE OF WHITE BEANS BAKED WITH MEATS

To serve 10 to 12

THE BEANS AND SAUSAGE
4 quarts chicken stock, fresh or
canned
2 pounds or 4 cups dry white beans
(Great Northern, marrow, or navy)
1 pound lean salt pork, in one piece
½ pound fresh pork rind (optional)
1 quart water
1 pound uncooked plain or garlic pork

sausage, fresh or smoked (French,
Italian or Polish)
3 whole peeled onions
1 teaspoon finely chopped garlic
1 teaspoon dried thyme, crumbled
Bouquet garni, made of 4 parsley
sprigs, 3 celery tops, white part of
1 leek, and 2 bay leaves, wrapped
and tied in cheesecloth
Salt
Freshly ground black pepper

THE BEANS AND SAUSAGE: In a heavy 6- to 8-quart pot or soup kettle, bring the chicken stock to a bubbling boil over high heat. Drop the beans in and boil them briskly for 2 minutes. Remove the pot from the heat and let the beans soak for 1 hour. Meanwhile, simmer the salt pork and optional pork rind in 1 quart of water for 15 minutes; drain and set aside.

With the point of a sharp knife, pierce 5 or 6 holes in the sausage; then add the sausage, salt pork and pork rind to the beans. Bring to a boil over high heat, skimming the top of scum. When the stock looks fairly clear, add the whole onions, garlic, thyme, *bouquet garni,* salt and a few grindings of black pepper. Reduce the heat and simmer uncovered for 45 minutes, adding stock or water if needed. With tongs, transfer the sausage to a plate and set it aside. Cook the beans and salt pork for another 30 to 40 minutes, or until the beans are tender, drain and transfer the salt pork and rind to the plate with the sausage; discard the onions and *bouquet garni.* Strain the stock through a large sieve or colander into a mixing bowl. Skim the fat from the stock and taste for seasoning. Then set the beans, stock and meats aside in separate containers. If they are to be kept overnight, cool, cover and refrigerate them.

THE DUCK
4 tablespoons soft butter

1 tablespoon vegetable oil
A 4- to 5-pound duck, quartered

THE BROILED DUCK: Preheat the oven to 350°. Cream the butter by beating it vigorously against the sides of a small bowl with a wooden spoon until it is fluffy, then beat in the oil. Dry the duck with paper towels, and coat the quarters with creamed butter and oil. Lay them skin side down on the broiler rack, and broil them 4 inches from the heat for 15 minutes, basting them once with pan juices, and broil 5 minutes more. Then increase the heat to 400° and broil for 15 minutes, basting the duck once or twice. With tongs, turn the quarters over, baste, and broil skin side up for 10

Continued on next page

minutes. Increase the heat to 450°, baste again, and broil for 10 minutes more. Remove the duck to a plate and pour the drippings from the broiler into a bowl, scraping in any browned bits that cling to the pan. Let the drippings settle, then skim the fat from the top and save it in a small bowl. Pour the degreased drippings into the bean stock. When the duck is cool, trim off the excess fat and gristle, and use poultry shears to cut the quarters into small serving pieces. If they are to be kept overnight, cool and cover the duck and bowl of fat and refrigerate them.

THE PORK AND LAMB

½ pound fresh pork fat, diced

1 pound boned pork loin, cut in
  2-inch chunks

1 pound boned lamb shoulder, cut in
  2-inch chunks

1 cup finely chopped onions

½ cup finely chopped celery

1 teaspoon finely chopped garlic

1 cup dry white wine

1½ pounds firm ripe tomatoes, peeled,
  seeded and coarsely chopped (about
  2 to 2½ cups) or substitute 2 cups
  chopped, drained, canned
  whole-pack tomatoes

1 bay leaf

½ teaspoon salt

Freshly ground black pepper

THE PORK AND LAMB: Preheat the oven to 325°. In a heavy 10- to 12-inch skillet, sauté the diced pork fat over moderate heat, stirring constantly, until crisp and brown. Remove the dice and reserve. Pour all but 2 or 3 tablespoons of rendered fat into a small mixing bowl. Heat the fat remaining in the skillet almost to the smoking point, and in it brown the pork and the lamb, 4 or 5 chunks at a time, adding more pork fat as needed. When the chunks are a rich brown on all sides, transfer them with tongs to a 4-quart Dutch oven or heavy flameproof casserole.

Now discard all but 3 tablespoons of fat from the skillet and cook the chopped onions over low heat for 5 minutes. Scrape in any browned bits clinging to the pan. Stir in the celery and garlic and cook for 2 minutes. Then pour in the wine, bring to a boil and cook over high heat until the mixture has been reduced to about half. With a rubber spatula, scrape the contents of the skillet into the casserole. Gently stir the tomatoes, bay leaf, salt and a few grindings of pepper into the casserole. Bring to a boil on top of the stove, cover, and bake on the middle shelf of the oven (adding a little stock or water if the meat looks dry) for 1 hour, or until the meat is tender. With tongs, transfer the meat to a bowl. If it is to be kept overnight, cool, cover and refrigerate. Skim the fat from the juices in the casserole, then strain the juices into the bean stock and discard the vegetables.

THE GRATIN TOPPING

1½ cups fine, dry bread crumbs   ½ cup finely chopped fresh parsley

ASSEMBLING THE CASSOULET: Preheat the oven to 350°. Peel the sausage and cut it into ¼-inch slices; cut the salt pork and pork rind into 1-inch squares. In a heavy flameproof 6- to 8-quart casserole at least 5 inches deep spread an inch-deep layer of beans. Arrange half of the sausage, salt pork, pork rind, diced pork fat, duck, braised pork and lamb on top. Cover with another layer of beans, then the rest of the meat, finally a last layer of beans, with a few slices of sausage on top. Slowly pour in the bean stock until it almost covers the beans. (If there isn't enough stock, add fresh or canned chicken stock.) Spread the bread crumbs in a thick layer on top and sprinkle them with 3 or 4 tablespoons of duck fat. Bring the casserole to a boil on top of the stove, then bake it uncovered in the upper third of the oven for 1¼ hours, or until the crumbs have formed a firm, dark crust. If desired, the first gratin, or crust, can be pushed gently into the *cassoulet*, and the dish baked until a new crust forms. This can be repeated two or three times if you wish. Serve directly from the casserole, sprinkled with parsley.

Gigot d'Agneau Rôti
ROAST LEG OF LAMB

To serve 6 to 8

	2 onions, thinly sliced
A 5- to 6-pound leg of lamb trimmed	2 carrots, thinly sliced
of excess fat but with the fell (or	1½ cups fresh or canned beef or
parchmentlike covering) left on	chicken stock
1 garlic clove, cut in slivers	½ teaspoon lemon juice
3 tablespoons vegetable oil	Salt
2 tablespoons salt	Freshly ground black pepper

Preheat the oven to 500°. Make 6 or 8 quarter-inch incisions on the fatty side of the lamb, and insert a sliver of garlic in each cut. Brush the leg with oil and pat salt all over it. Insert a meat thermometer into the thickest part of the leg, being careful not to touch a bone. Place the leg, fat side up, on a rack in a shallow roasting pan and roast it uncovered for 20 minutes on the middle shelf of the oven. Then reduce the heat to 375°, scatter the vegetables around the rack and roast the lamb for another 40 to 60 minutes, or until done to your liking. For rare lamb, roast it until the meat thermometer reads 130° to 140°, for medium, 140° to 150°; for well done, 150° to 160°. Transfer the lamb to a heated platter and remove the thermometer; let it rest 10 minutes before carving.

Meanwhile, skim off the fat from the roasting pan, add the stock to the vegetables and boil briskly on top of the stove for 4 or 5 minutes, scraping in any browned bits clinging to the pan. When the sauce has reached the intensity of flavor desired, strain it through a fine sieve into a saucepan, pressing down hard on the vegetables before discarding them. Skim the sauce of its surface fat; taste the sauce and season it with lemon juice, salt and pepper. Reheat the sauce and serve it with the lamb.

Côtes de Veau à l'Ardennaise
BRAISED VEAL CHOPS WITH HAM AND PARSLEY DRESSING

To serve 4

5 tablespoons butter
½ cup finely chopped onions
¼ cup finely chopped carrots
10 juniper berries
½ teaspoon dried basil
½ teaspoon salt
Freshly ground black pepper
3 tablespoons vegetable oil
4 veal loin chops, cut 1 to 1½ inches
    thick
1 cup dry white wine

½ cup chicken stock, fresh or canned
¾ cup fresh white bread crumbs,
    made in a blender from about 3
    slices of white bread with crusts
    removed
1 tablespoon finely chopped boiled
    ham
2 tablespoons finely chopped fresh
    parsley
½ teaspoon lemon juice
1 tablespoon butter, cut in tiny
    pieces

Preheat the oven to 350°. In a heavy shallow flameproof casserole or baking dish that is large enough to hold the chops in one layer and has a cover, melt 2 tablespoons of the butter over moderate heat, and in it cook the chopped onions and carrots, stirring occasionally, for 8 to 10 minutes, or until limp and lightly colored. Set aside.

With a mortar and pestle or a wooden spoon and small, heavy mixing bowl, crush the juniper berries and mash in the basil, salt and a few gridings of pepper. Press the juniper-berry seasoning into both sides of the chops, forcing it into the meat as much as possible.

Melt 1 tablespoon of the butter with the oil in a heavy 10- to 12-inch skillet over moderate heat. When the foam subsides, brown the chops to a rich golden color on both sides, turning them carefully to avoid dislodging the seasoning. Transfer the browned chops to the casserole. Pour off all but 1 or 2 tablespoons of fat from the skillet and add the wine. Boil briskly, stirring and scraping in any browned bits that cling to the pan, until the wine has been reduced to ½ cup; then stir in the stock and pour the mixture around the veal chops. In a 6- to 8-inch skillet, melt the remaining 2 tablespoons of butter over low heat, and cook the bread crumbs until they are lightly browned. Off the heat, stir in the ham, parsley and ½ teaspoon of lemon juice. Divide the mixture into quarters, and spoon a portion onto each chop. Dot the topping with butter.

Bring the casserole to a boil on top of the stove, cover tightly and bake for 40 minutes. Then transfer the veal to a heated platter, preferably one with a well to catch the sauce. Working quickly, strain the contents of the casserole through a fine sieve into a small saucepan, pressing down hard on the vegetables with the back of a spoon before discarding them. Boil down the liquids over high heat until they are reduced to about ½ cup. Taste the sauce for seasoning, pour it around the chops and serve at once.

Ris de Veau ou Cervelles au Beurre Noir

SWEETBREADS OR BRAINS IN BROWN BUTTER SAUCE

To serve 6

1½ pounds calf's sweetbreads or brains
Water
Vinegar
Salt
Lemon juice
15 tablespoons butter (almost ½

pound)
¼ cup wine vinegar or lemon juice
Freshly ground black pepper
Flour
3 tablespoons butter
1 tablespoon vegetable oil
2 tablespoons finely chopped fresh
  parsley

Soak the sweetbreads or brains in several changes of cold water for 2 hours; then soak them for another hour in acidulated cold water, using one tablespoon of vinegar for each quart of water. Gently pull off as much of the outside membrane as possible without tearing the brains or sweetbreads. Trim the sweetbreads by cutting the two lobes from the tube between them with a small sharp knife; discard the tubes. Trim the brains by cutting off the white, opaque bits at the base. Place the sweetbreads or brains in an enameled saucepan with enough water to cover by 2 inches, add the salt (1 teaspoon per quart of water) and lemon juice (1 tablespoon per quart of water), and cook uncovered just below a simmer for 15 to 20 minutes. Spread the sweetbreads or brains on paper towels to dry.

Clarify 12 tablespoons of the butter in a small heavy saucepan or skillet by melting it slowly, skimming off the surface foam. Spoon the clear butter on top into a clean pan and discard the milky residue. Pour the vinegar into the pan in which the butter melted and boil it briskly until it has been reduced to 1 tablespoon. Over moderate heat, brown the clarified butter. Stir in the reduced vinegar, taste and season with salt and pepper.

If the sweetbreads or brains are to be served whole, add them to the brown butter sauce and, basting periodically, heat through. If they are to be sliced and sautéed, set the brown butter sauce aside. Dip the slices in flour, then shake off all but a fine dusting of flour. In a heavy 10- to 12-inch skillet or sauté pan, melt the remaining 3 tablespoons of butter with the oil over moderate heat. When the foam subsides, sauté the sliced sweetbreads or brains 3 or 4 minutes on each side, or until lightly browned. If all the slices don't fit into the skillet easily, sauté them in two batches. Arrange the slices neatly on a heated platter. Reheat the brown butter and pour it over them. Sprinkle with chopped parsley and serve at once.

Côtes de Porc à l'Auvergnate
PORK CHOPS BAKED WITH CABBAGE

To serve 4

6 quarts water
Salt
3 pounds cabbage, finely chopped
   (about 12 cups)
3 tablespoons butter
½ cup finely chopped onions
½ teaspoon finely chopped garlic
Freshly ground black pepper

8 center-cut loin pork chops, about
   ¾ inch thick
3 tablespoons oil
½ cup dry white wine
1 cup heavy cream
1 bay leaf
4 teaspoons freshly grated Parmesan
   cheese mixed with 2 teaspoons
   fine, dry bread crumbs

In a soup pot or kettle, bring the water and 3 tablespoons of salt to a bubbling boil. Drop in the cabbage and boil for 5 minutes. Drain the cabbage thoroughly in a sieve or colander. In a 10- to 12-inch skillet, melt 2 tablespoons of the butter over moderate heat. When the foam subsides, cook the onions and garlic, stirring constantly, for 3 or 4 minutes, or until they are soft but not brown. Stir in the cabbage, ½ teaspoon salt and a few grindings of pepper, and cook, stirring frequently, for 5 minutes, or until almost all of the moisture in the pan has evaporated. With a rubber spatula, transfer the contents of the skillet to a bowl; set aside.

Pat the pork chops dry with paper towels, and season them with salt and a few grindings of black pepper. In the skillet, melt the remaining 1 tablespoon of butter with the oil over moderate heat. When the foam subsides, brown the chops for about 3 minutes on each side, or until they are a rich golden color. Remove them from the skillet with tongs and set them aside. Pour off almost all the fat from the skillet, leaving only a thin film on the bottom. Add the wine and boil rapidly, stirring frequently and scraping in any brown bits that cling to the bottom and sides of the pan, until the wine is reduced to ¼ cup. Mix the reduced wine into the cabbage. Spread about ⅓ of the cabbage in the bottom of a heavy flameproof casserole at least 4 inches deep, and large enough to hold 4 chops in a single layer. Lay 4 chops on top of the cabbage, then add another layer of cabbage, 4 more chops, and finish with the rest of the cabbage. The casserole should be firmly packed. Preheat the oven to 350°.

In a small saucepan, scald the cream by heating it over moderate heat until tiny bubbles form around the edge of the pan. Pour the hot cream into the casserole and place a bay leaf on top of the cabbage. Bring the casserole to a simmer on top of the stove, then set it into a larger pan to catch any juices that may spill over during cooking, cover it tightly, and bake it on the middle shelf of the oven for 1½ hours. Remove the cover, discard the bay leaf and check the seasoning. Sprinkle the cabbage with cheese and crumbs. Bake the casserole for 30 minutes longer, or until the top is browned and crusty. Serve directly from the casserole.

Rognons en Casserole
SAUTÉED KIDNEYS WITH MUSTARD SAUCE

To serve 4 to 6

6 tablespoons butter
3 or 4 whole veal kidneys or 12 whole lamb kidneys, peeled and trimmed of fat
2 tablespoons finely chopped shallots or scallions
¾ cup dry white wine

4 tablespoons soft butter
2 tablespoons Dijon-style prepared mustard
½ teaspoon salt
Freshly ground black pepper
2 teaspoons lemon juice
3 tablespoons finely chopped fresh parsley

In a heavy, shallow flameproof casserole about 10 inches across, or in a chafing dish, melt the 6 tablespoons of butter over moderate heat. When the foam subsides, sauté the kidneys in the butter, uncovered, turning them frequently, until they are lightly browned. (Sauté veal kidneys for 10 minutes, lamb kidneys for 4 to 5.) With tongs, transfer the kidneys to a heated platter and cover loosely to keep them warm.

Stir the shallots into the butter remaining in the casserole and cook, stirring, for 1 minute. Then add the wine and bring to a boil, stirring constantly and scraping in any brown bits or coagulated juices that cling to the pan. Boil briskly for 4 to 5 minutes or until the wine is reduced to ¼ cup. Remove the casserole from the heat. Cream the butter by beating it vigorously with a wooden spoon until it is fluffy, then beat in the mustard, salt and a few grindings of pepper. Off the heat, swirl spoonfuls of the seasoned butter into the casserole.

Working quickly, cut the kidneys into crosswise slices ⅛ inch thick. Return them to the casserole, sprinkle with lemon juice and parsley, and toss over low heat for 1 or 2 minutes to heat them through. Serve at once.

Bifteck Marchand de Vins

SAUTÉED STEAK WITH RED WINE SAUCE

To serve 6

MARCHAND DE VINS SAUCE
2 tablespoons butter
½ cup finely chopped shallots or
    scallions
1½ cups dry red wine
½ bay leaf
¼ teaspoon dried thyme

4 parsley sprigs
2 teaspoons meat extract combined
    with 3 tablespoons hot water
12 tablespoons soft butter (1½
    quarter-pound sticks)
1 tablespoon lemon juice
1 teaspoon flour
2 tablespoons finely chopped fresh
    parsley

MARCHAND DE VINS SAUCE: In a 1- to 2-quart enameled saucepan, melt 2 tablespoons of butter over moderate heat. When the foam subsides, cook the shallots, stirring constantly, for 2 minutes, or until they are soft but not brown. Pour in the wine, add the bay leaf, thyme and parsley sprigs and simmer over moderate heat until reduced to ¾ cup. This process may take 10 to 15 minutes. Strain the reduced wine through a fine sieve into a small bowl, pressing down hard on the shallots and herbs with the back of a spoon before discarding them. Return the wine to the saucepan, add the thinned meat extract and bring to a boil. Set the pan aside.

Cream 12 tablespoons of soft butter, beating it vigorously against the side of a small bowl with a wooden spoon until it is fluffy. Beat in the lemon juice, flour and parsley. Set the bowl aside.

THE STEAK
A 3- to 3½-pound sirloin, porterhouse
    or T-bone steak, cut 1 to 1¼
    inch thick and trimmed of excess
    fat

1 tablespoon butter
2 tablespoons vegetable oil
Salt
Freshly ground black pepper

THE STEAK: Pat the steak thoroughly dry with paper towels. Cut small incisions every inch or so around the outside of the steak so the fat won't curl as it cooks. In a heavy 12- or 14-inch skillet or sauté pan, melt 1 tablespoon of butter with the 2 tablespoons of vegetable oil over high heat. Add the steak and brown it quickly for 1 or 2 minutes on each side, turning it with tongs. Then reduce the heat to moderate and sauté the steak for about 5 minutes on each side, or until it is done to a medium-rare degree.

Experts test a steak by pressing it with a finger. It should be slightly resilient, neither soft nor firm. If that method seems tricky, make a small incision near the bone with the tip of a sharp knife and judge by the meat's color. Transfer to a heated platter and season with salt and pepper.

Pour the reduced wine mixture into the skillet and bring it to a boil over moderate heat, stirring constantly and scraping in any browned bits that cling to the bottom and sides of the pan. Remove from the heat and blend in the creamed butter mixture, 2 tablespoons at a time. To serve, slice the steak and offer the sauce separately.

ALTERNATIVE: *Sauce béarnaise (page 14)* can take the place of the *marchand de vins* sauce. In this case, the name of the dish becomes *bifteck béarnaise*.

Veau Braisé en Casserole
CASSEROLE-ROASTED VEAL

To serve 6

2 tablespoons butter
2 tablespoons vegetable oil
A 3-pound boneless veal rump,
   shoulder or loin roast, wrapped in
   a thin layer of fat and tied
2 carrots, thinly sliced

2 onions, thinly sliced
½ teaspoon salt
Freshly ground black pepper
Bouquet garni made of 4 parsley sprigs
   and 1 bay leaf, tied together
½ teaspoon dried thyme, crumbled
½ cup hot chicken stock, fresh or
   canned (optional)

Preheat the oven to 325°. In a heavy casserole that is just large enough to hold the veal and has a cover, melt the butter with the oil over moderate heat. When the foam subsides, brown the veal lightly on all sides. Remove the veal to a plate and stir the vegetables into the fat remaining in the casserole. (If the fat has burned, discard it and use 3 tablespoons of fresh butter instead.) Cook the vegetables over low heat for 5 to 10 minutes, stirring occasionally, until they are tender but not brown.

Return the veal to the casserole, sprinkle it with salt and a few grindings of pepper, and add the *bouquet garni* and the thyme. Cover the casserole and bring it to a sizzle on top of the stove, then place it in the lower third of the oven. Using a bulb baster or large spoon, baste the veal every 20 or 30 minutes with the juices that will accumulate in the pan. In the unlikely event the casserole is dry, add the hot chicken stock. After 1½ hours test the veal for doneness by piercing it with the tip of a sharp knife—the juices should run clear yellow. Transfer the veal to a heated platter and cut off the strings. Strain the juices remaining in the casserole through a fine sieve into a small saucepan, pressing down hard on the vegetables and herbs with a spoon to extract their juices before discarding them. Skim the fat from the top and boil the liquid down to about half its original volume, or until it reaches the intensity of flavor desired. Taste for seasoning. Carve the veal into ¼-inch slices, moisten each slice with a little of the roasting juices and pass the rest in a warm sauceboat.

Côtes de Porc Braisées à la Moutarde

BRAISED PORK CHOPS WITH CREAM AND MUSTARD SAUCE

To serve 6

6 center cut loin pork chops, cut 1½
  inches thick
Salt
Freshly ground black pepper
Flour
2 tablespoons butter
3 tablespoons vegetable oil
1½ cups thinly sliced onions

3 tablespoons wine vinegar
  (preferably white)
Bouquet garni made of 2 parsley
  sprigs and 1 bay leaf, tied together
¾ cup heavy cream
2 teaspoons Dijon-style prepared
  mustard
A few drops of lemon juice
Fresh parsley sprigs

Preheat the oven to 325°. Season the chops generously with salt and pepper, dip them in flour, then vigorously shake off all but a light dusting. In a heavy 10- to 12-inch skillet, melt the butter with the oil over moderate heat. When the foam subsides, brown the chops for about 3 minutes on each side, or until they are a rich golden color. As the chops brown, remove them from the skillet with tongs and place them in a shallow flameproof casserole large enough to hold them all, preferably in one layer.

After the chops are browned, pour off all but a thin film of fat from the skillet. Add the onions and cook them over moderate heat, stirring frequently, for 5 minutes, or until they are soft and lightly browned. Stir in the wine vinegar, bring it to a boil and scrape up any browned bits that cling to the bottom and sides of the skillet. Cook the vinegar almost completely away, then spoon the onions and juices over the chops, and add the *bouquet garni*.

Bring the casserole to a sizzle on top of the stove, cover it tightly and bake it on the middle shelf of the oven for 10 minutes. With a bulb baster or large spoon, baste the chops with the juices that have accumulated in the casserole or, if there is not enough of these, with 2 or 3 tablespoons of heated chicken stock. Bake for 10 minutes longer, then turn the chops over and baste them again. After another 10 minutes, test the chops by piercing one near the bone with the tip of a sharp knife; if the juices that run out are yellow with no traces of pink, the chops are done. With tongs, transfer the chops to a heated platter and cover or set in a 200° oven to keep warm.

Tip the casserole and skim as much fat as possible from the surface of the drippings. Pour in the cream and bring the sauce to a boil over high heat, stirring constantly. When the sauce has thickened sufficiently to coat the back of a spoon lightly, remove the casserole from the heat and stir in the mustard and lemon juice. Strain the sauce through a fine sieve directly over the chops, pressing down hard on the onions with the back of a spoon before discarding them. Garnish the chops with parsley and serve at once.

Navarin Printanier

LAMB STEW WITH SPRING VEGETABLES

To serve 6 to 8

1/2 cup vegetable oil
4 pounds boneless lean lamb, cut in
   2-inch chunks
3 tablespoons flour
1 teaspoon dried thyme, crumbled
1 teaspoon salt
Freshly ground black pepper

1/4 cup finely chopped shallots or
   scallions
1 teaspoon finely chopped garlic
3 cups beef stock, fresh or canned
1 cup peeled, seeded and coarsely
   chopped fresh tomatoes
Bouquet garni made of 4 parsley
   sprigs, white part of 1 leek, and 1
   bay leaf, tied together

Preheat the oven to 500°. In a heavy 10- to 12-inch skillet heat 2 tablespoons of oil almost to the smoking point. Brown the lamb, 4 or 5 chunks at a time, adding more oil as needed. When the chunks are a rich brown on all sides, remove them with tongs to a Dutch oven or a heavy 6- to 8-quart flameproof casserole. Pour off almost all the fat from the skillet and set it aside.

Sprinkle the browned lamb with flour, thyme, salt and a few grindings of pepper, tossing the meat to coat it as evenly as possible. Place the casserole, uncovered, in the upper third of the oven, and cook the lamb, turning it every few minutes, for 8 to 10 minutes, or until the chunks are slightly crusted and there is no trace of gummy flour. Remove the casserole from the oven and set aside. Reduce the oven heat to 325°.

In the fat remaining in the skillet, cook the shallots and garlic over moderately low heat for about 2 minutes, stirring constantly. Pour in the beef stock and bring to a boil, stirring constantly and scraping in any brown bits that cling to the bottom and sides of the pan. Add the tomatoes and stir once more, then pour the sauce over the lamb, mixing gently with a spoon. Add the *bouquet garni,* bring the casserole to a boil on top of the stove, cover it tightly, and place it on the middle shelf of the oven to simmer for 45 minutes, or until the lamb is nearly tender when pierced with the tip of a sharp knife.

VEGETABLE GARNISH

6 tablespoons butter
12 to 16 peeled white onions, about
   1 inch in diameter
6 to 8 carrots, peeled and cut in
   2-inch cylinders or olive shapes
6 medium white turnips, peeled and
   cut in quarters
12 to 16 small new potatoes, peeled
2 quarts water

1 pound fresh green peas, shelled
   (about 1 cup) or 1 ten-ounce
   package defrosted frozen peas
1/2 pound fresh green beans, cut in
   1-inch lengths (about 1 1/2 cups), or
   1 ten-ounce package defrosted
   frozen cut beans
2 tablespoons finely chopped fresh
   parsley

Continued on next page

VEGETABLE GARNISH: Meanwhile, in a heavy 10- to 12-inch skillet, melt 6 tablespoons of butter. When the foam subsides, add the onions, carrots, turnips and potatoes, and cook them over moderate heat, stirring occasionally, for 7 to 8 minutes, or until they are coated with butter and lightly browned. Set them aside. Bring the water to a bubbling boil in a 3- to 4-quart saucepan, add the fresh peas and beans, and boil them briskly uncovered for about 10 minutes, or until the beans are barely tender. Immediately drain them in a sieve and plunge the sieve into cold water for a minute or so. Set them aside. If you are substituting defrosted frozen peas, it is not necessary to cook them; they will be heated through and briefly cooked later. Defrosted frozen beans, on the other hand, should be simmered in a little water for 3 to 4 minutes.

After the lamb has cooked for 45 minutes, strain the entire contents of the casserole through a large fine sieve into a mixing bowl. While the braising liquid or sauce is draining, wash the casserole and spread the onions, carrots, turnips and potatoes in the bottom. With tongs, pick the pieces of lamb out of the sieve, and arrange them over the vegetables. Skim off the fat and taste the sauce for seasoning; then pour it over the meat and vegetables in the casserole. Bring to a boil on top of the stove, cover tightly, and return to the oven for another 20 minutes. Gently stir in the peas and green beans and cook for about 10 minutes longer, or until the lamb and vegetables are tender.

Serve the *navarin* directly from the casserole, garnished with chopped parsley. For a more formal dinner, mound the lamb in the center of a large, deep, heated platter and surround it with vegetables; moisten everything well with sauce and garnish the meat with parsley. Pour the rest of the sauce into a warm sauceboat and serve it separately.

Carbonades de Boeuf à la Flamande
BEEF AND ONIONS BRAISED IN BEER

To serve 6 to 8

¼ pound salt pork, diced
2 cups water
5 tablespoons butter
7 cups thinly sliced onions (about 2
    pounds)
3 pounds lean boneless beef chuck
    or rump, cut in 2-inch chunks
Bouquet garni made of 4 parsley
    sprigs and 1 bay leaf, tied together

3 tablespoons flour
2 cups beer
1½ cups beef stock, fresh or canned
1½ teaspoons sugar
1 tablespoon vinegar
1 teaspoon finely chopped garlic
1 teaspoon dried thyme, crumbled
Salt
Freshly ground black pepper
2 tablespoons finely chopped fresh
    parsley

To remove excess saltiness, blanch the pork dice by simmering them in 2 cups of water for 5 minutes, drain on paper towels and pat dry. In a heavy 10- to 12-inch skillet, melt 1 tablespoon of the butter over moderate heat, and in it brown the pork dice, stirring them or shaking the pan frequently, until they are crisp and golden. Remove them with a slotted spoon and set them aside to drain on paper towels. Pour off almost all the rendered fat from the skillet into a small bowl, leaving just enough in the skillet to make a thin film about 1/16 inch deep on the bottom. Set the bowl of fat and the skillet aside.

In another heavy 10- to 12-inch skillet, melt 4 tablespoons of butter over moderate heat. When the foam subsides, add the sliced onions and cook them over low heat, turning them frequently with a wide metal spatula, for 20 to 30 minutes, or until they become limp and lightly colored.

While the onions are cooking, heat the fat in the first skillet over moderate heat until it almost smokes. Dry the beef with paper towels, then brown it in the hot oil 4 or 5 chunks at a time to avoid crowding the skillet, adding more pork fat as needed. When the chunks are a rich brown on all sides, remove them with kitchen tongs to a Dutch oven or a heavy, flameproof casserole about 9 to 10 inches in diameter and at least 3 inches deep. Bury the *bouquet garni* in the meat.

Preheat the oven to 350°. After all the meat is browned, remove the skillet from the heat and stir the flour into the fat remaining in it. If the mixture seems dry, add a little more pork fat (or vegetable oil). Return to very low heat and cook, stirring constantly, until the *roux* is amber color: be careful it doesn't burn. Remove from heat, pour in the beer and beef stock, and beat vigorously with a wire whisk until the *roux* and liquid are blended. Bring to a boil over moderate heat, whisking constantly as the sauce thickens. Boil for 1 minute, then mix in the sugar, vinegar, garlic and thyme, and simmer over low heat for 2 or 3 minutes. Taste the sauce and season it with salt and pepper if needed.

When the onions are done, add them to the casserole, and pour the sauce over the onions and meat, stirring the mixture gently. The sauce should nearly cover the meat; add more beer if needed. Bring the casserole to a boil on top of the stove, cover it tightly and place it in the lower third of the oven. Cook, regulating the oven heat so that the meat simmers slowly for 1½ to 2 hours, or until the meat is tender when pierced with the tip of a sharp knife. Before serving, let the *carbonades* cool for a few minutes. Then skim off the surface fat, discard the *bouquet garni* and taste the sauce for seasoning. Sprinkle the *carbonades* with the crisp pork bits and garnish with chopped parsley.

Blanquette de Veau à l'Ancienne

OLD-FASHIONED VEAL STEW WITH CREAM SAUCE

To serve 6

3 to 3½ pounds boneless veal shoulder
  cut into 2-inch chunks
Water
6⅔ cups chicken stock, fresh or
  canned
2 carrots, peeled and cut in chunks
1 large whole peeled onion
2 celery tops
1 leek, white part plus 2 inches of
  green (optional)
1 teaspoon dried thyme
1 bay leaf
4 parsley sprigs

1 teaspoon salt
5 tablespoons butter
18 peeled white onions, about 1 inch
  in diameter
1 pound fresh mushrooms, whole if
  small, quartered or sliced if large
1 teaspoon lemon juice
3 tablespoons flour
2 egg yolks
1 cup heavy cream
Salt
White pepper
2 tablespoons finely chopped fresh
  parsley

In a heavy 4- to 6-quart casserole, blanch the veal by covering it with cold water, bringing it to a boil over high heat and boiling it briskly for 1 minute. Drain the veal immediately. Under cold running water, wash away any accumulated scum. Wash the casserole and return the veal to it. Add 6 cups of the chicken stock, carrots, onion, celery, leek, herbs and salt. The meat should be completely covered with liquid; add more stock or water if needed. Bring to a boil over moderate heat, skimming off any scum. Reduce the heat to low and simmer the veal, partially covered, for 1 to 1½ hours, or until it is tender when pierced with a sharp knife.

While the veal is simmering, combine the remaining ⅔ cup chicken stock, 2 tablespoons of the butter, and the onions in a 10- to 12-inch enameled or stainless-steel skillet. Bring to a boil, cover and simmer, stirring occasionally, for 15 to 20 minutes, or until the onions are tender. With a slotted spoon, transfer them to a bowl. Stir the mushrooms and lemon juice into the stock remaining in the skillet. Bring to a boil, cover and simmer for 5 minutes. With a slotted spoon, remove them from the pan and add them to the onions. Pour the liquid remaining in the skillet into the simmering casserole.

When the veal is tender, transfer it to a bowl with a slotted spoon. Strain the stock from the casserole through a fine sieve into a 2- to 3-quart saucepan, pressing down hard on the vegetables and herbs with the back of a spoon before discarding them. Skim off the surface fat. Over high heat, boil the stock down until it has been reduced to about half.

In a small saucepan, melt the remaining 3 tablespoons of butter over moderate heat, and stir in the flour. Return to low heat and cook, stirring constantly, for 2 minutes. Do not let this *roux* brown. Remove from heat, pour in 2 cups of reduced stock and blend vigorously with a wire whisk. Then return to high heat and cook the sauce, stirring constantly, until it thickens and comes to a boil. Reduce the heat and simmer for about 10 minutes, skimming off any scum.

Remove from the heat. With a wire whisk, blend the egg yolks and cream together in a bowl. Whisk in the hot sauce, 2 tablespoons at a time, until ½ cup has been added; then reverse the process and whisk the egg-yolk-and-cream mixture back into the remaining hot sauce. Bring it to a boil, stirring constantly; then boil slowly for 30 seconds. Taste and season with salt, white pepper and a few drops of lemon juice.

Drain the veal, onions and mushrooms of any juices that may have accumulated in their bowls. Wash the casserole and spread the veal and vegetables in it. Pour the sauce over them and gently stir to coat every piece. Simmer over moderate heat for 5 to 10 minutes, or until the veal is thoroughly heated. Do not let the sauce boil again. Sprinkle with parsley, and serve directly from the casserole.

Foie de Veau Sauté

SAUTÉED CALF'S LIVER

To serve 6

6 slices of calf's liver, cut ½ inch thick (about 1½ pounds)
Salt
Freshly ground black pepper
Flour
4 tablespoons butter

2 tablespoons vegetable oil
½ cup beef or chicken stock, fresh or canned
1 tablespoon soft butter
A few drops of lemon juice
2 tablespoons finely chopped, fresh parsley

Season the liver slices with salt and a few grindings of pepper. Dip the slices in flour, then vigorously shake off all but a fine dusting. In a heavy 12-inch skillet or sauté pan, melt the butter with the oil over high heat. When the foam subsides, sauté the liver quickly for 2 or 3 minutes on each side, turning the slices with kitchen tongs. Remove the liver to a heated platter and cover loosely to keep warm.

Working quickly, pour off almost all the fat from the skillet, leaving just enough to film the bottom. Add the chicken stock and cook over high heat, stirring constantly and scraping in any brown bits that cling to the pan.

Continue to cook until the stock is syrupy and has been reduced to about ¼ cup. Remove the pan from the heat and swirl in 1 tablespoon of soft butter and a few drops of lemon juice. Pour the sauce over the liver, sprinkle with parsley and serve at once.

Sauté de Veau Marengo
VEAL STEW WITH TOMATOES AND MUSHROOMS

To serve 6 to 8

3 pounds boned shoulder of veal,
   trimmed and cut into 2-inch
   chunks
4 tablespoons olive or vegetable oil
1 teaspoon dried thyme, crumbled
1 teaspoon salt
Freshly ground black pepper
2 tablespoons flour
2 tablespoons butter
1 cup finely chopped onions
½ teaspoon finely chopped garlic

½ cup dry white wine
1½ cups beef stock, fresh or canned
1 cup peeled, seeded and coarsely
   chopped tomatoes, or drained
   canned tomatoes
2 two-inch strips fresh lemon peel
Bouquet garni made of 4 parsley
   sprigs and 1 bay leaf, tied together
3 tablespoons butter
¾ pound fresh mushrooms, whole if
   small, sliced or quartered if large
2 tablespoons finely chopped fresh
   parsley

Preheat the oven to 500°. Dry the veal with paper towels. In a heavy 10- to 12-inch skillet, heat the oil to the smoking point. Add the veal 4 or 5 chunks at a time and sauté until a rich, golden brown on all sides, then transfer to a heavy 4- to 5-quart casserole. When all the veal is browned, discard the cooking oil and, without washing the skillet, set it aside. Sprinkle the browned veal with thyme, salt, a little pepper and then with flour, tossing the meat to coat it as evenly as possible. Place the casserole uncovered in the upper third of the oven and cook the veal, turning it 2 or 3 times, for 8 to 10 minutes, or until the chunks are slightly crusted and there is no trace of gummy flour. Remove from the oven. Reduce the oven heat to 325°.

Melt 2 tablespoons of butter in the waiting skillet over low heat and in it cook the chopped onions and garlic, scraping in any browned bits that cling to the bottom and sides of the pan, for 10 minutes, or until the onions are soft and lightly browned. Add the wine and beef stock, and bring to a boil over high heat. Boil for 1 or 2 minutes, then pour into the casserole, scraping the skillet clean. Stir in the tomatoes, lemon peel and *bouquet garni.*

Bring the casserole to a boil on top of the stove, cover tightly and cook on the middle shelf of the oven 1 to 1¼ hours, or until the veal is tender when pierced with the tip of a sharp knife. Meanwhile, melt 3 tablespoons of butter in an 8- to 10-inch enameled or stainless-steel skillet. Add the mushrooms and toss them in the butter for 3 minutes, turning them constantly with a wooden spoon. When the veal is done, gently stir the mushrooms and whatever liquid has collected in the skillet into the casserole, and continue cooking for 10 or 15 minutes.

Remove the casserole from the oven and ladle the entire contents into a large, fine sieve set over a 2- to 3-quart saucepan. After the sauce drains through, discard the lemon peel and *bouquet garni*. Wash the casserole and return the veal and mushrooms to it. Skim as much fat as possible from the drained sauce, and bring it to a boil over high heat. When it has cooked down to about 2 cups, taste it for seasoning, then pour the sauce over the veal and, just before serving, simmer it for 5 to 10 minutes. Serve the veal directly from the casserole or arranged attractively on a large heated platter. Garnish it with chopped parsley.

Escalopes de Veau à la Savoyarde
SAUTÉED VEAL SCALLOPS WITH CREAM SAUCE

To serve 4

8 veal scallops, cut ½ inch thick and pounded ¼ inch thick (1½ to 2 pounds)
Salt
Freshly ground black pepper
Flour

3 tablespoons butter
1 tablespoon vegetable oil
2 tablespoons finely chopped shallots or scallions
½ cup dry white wine
½ cup heavy cream
A few drops of lemon juice
Fresh parsley sprigs

Season the scallops with salt and a few grindings of pepper. Dip them in flour and then shake them vigorously to remove all but a light dusting. In a 10- to 12-inch enameled or stainless-steel skillet, melt the butter with the oil over moderate heat. When the foam subsides, brown the scallops for 3 or 4 minutes on each side, or until they are a light golden color. Remove them from the pan and set aside. Pour off almost all the fat from the skillet, leaving just enough to make a thin film on the bottom. Stir in the shallots and cook slowly for a moment. Pour in the wine and bring it to a boil over high heat, stirring and scraping in any browned bits that cling to the bottom or sides of the pan. Boil for 2 or 3 minutes until the wine has been reduced to about ¼ cup. Reduce the heat, stir in the cream and simmer, stirring constantly, for 3 to 5 minutes, or until the sauce thickens. Taste and season with a few drops of lemon juice, salt and pepper. Return the scallops to the skillet, baste with the sauce and cook just long enough to heat the scallops through. Arrange the scallops, overlapping them slightly, down the center of a heated serving platter, pour the sauce over them, decorate with parsley and serve at once.

Tripes à la Mode de Caen

CASSEROLE OF TRIPE

To serve 8 to 10

5 pounds ready-to-cook tripe
4 ready-to-cook calf's feet, split in
    half and boned, or 2 sawed veal
    knuckles and an 8- by 3-inch piece
    of fresh or salt pork rind
3 onions, peeled and cut in half
3 carrots, peeled and cut in chunks
4 leeks, whites plus 2 inches of green,
    split, or substitute 2 more onions,
    cut in half
Bouquet garni made of 6 parsley

sprigs, 2 bay leaves, 5 peeled garlic
    cloves, 1 teaspoon dried thyme and
    15 peppercorns, tied together in
    washed cheesecloth
1½ tablespoons salt
3 cups dry white wine
3 cups chicken stock, fresh or canned
1½ cups Calvados or applejack
½ pound beef fat, sliced in ⅛-inch
    sheets
2 tablespoons finely chopped fresh
    parsley

With a sharp knife, cut the sheets of tripe into 1½-inch squares. Wash them in a large bowl set under a slow trickle of cold tap water until the water in the bowl is clear. Drain thoroughly in a colander or large sieve. Meanwhile, blanch the calf's feet (or veal knuckles and pork rind) in a large saucepan or soup kettle by covering them with cold water, bringing the water to a boil over high heat and cooking them briskly for 2 minutes. Drain the feet in a colander and rinse thoroughly in cold water.

Preheat the oven to 250°. Spread the onions, carrots, leeks and *bouquet garni* in the bottom of a heavy flameproof 6- to 8-quart casserole that has a tight cover. Lay the tripe over them and salt it. Place the calf's feet (or veal knuckles and pork rind) on top and pour in the wine, stock and Calvados. (Unsweet cider, instead of wine, is traditional in Caen. If your liquor store has it, you may substitute imported dry hard cider—not apple juice or sweetened cider—for the wine.) Add more stock or water if necessary to cover the ingredients. Drape the sheets of beef fat loosely over the top. Seal the casserole with a double layer of aluminum foil folded down over the sides and tied in place, then cover the casserole. Bring to a simmer on top of the stove; set the casserole in a large roasting pan to catch any overflow and place it on the middle shelf of the oven to bake for at least 12 hours—up to 16 hours if you wish.

When the tripe is done, remove the casserole from the oven, uncover it and peel off the foil. With tongs, remove and discard the calf's feet (or veal knuckles and pork rind), vegetables and *bouquet garni;* pour the tripe and all its juices into a fine sieve set over a large mixing bowl. After the tripe has drained, transfer it to a 3- to 4-quart casserole. Let the sauce from the tripe settle for 5 minutes, then skim as much fat as possible from the surface. Taste the sauce for seasoning, pour it over the tripe and bring the casserole to a simmer on top of the stove. Sprinkle with parsley and serve at once. It is important that tripe be served on heated plates because the sauce will thicken to a jelly if the plates are the slightest bit cool.

Choucroute Garnie
BRAISED SAUERKRAUT WITH MEAT

To serve 6

4 pounds fresh sauerkraut
1½ pounds lean salt pork in 1 piece
2 quarts water
6 tablespoons lard
2½ cups finely chopped onions
1 cup 2-inch carrot chunks
1 teaspoon finely chopped garlic
1 large tart apple, peeled, cored and
   coarsely chopped
3 cups chicken stock, fresh or canned
2 cups dry white wine
½ teaspoon salt

Freshly ground black pepper
Bouquet garni made of 4 parsley
   sprigs, 1 bay leaf and 10 juniper
   berries, tied together in washed
   cheesecloth (or add ¼ cup gin to the
   casserole to substitute for the
   juniper berries)
1½ pounds uncooked plain or garlic
   pork sausage, fresh or smoked
   (French, Italian or Polish)
6 slices smoked baked ham cut ¼
   inch thick
6 whole, peeled potatoes, boiled just
   before serving time

Wash the sauerkraut in several changes of water to get rid of excess saltiness, then squeeze it vigorously to dry it. Blanch the salt pork by simmering it in 2 quarts of water for 15 minutes; drain and set aside.

Preheat the oven to 325°. In a heavy 4-quart flameproof casserole that has a cover, melt the lard over moderate heat. Add the onions, carrots and garlic, and cook, stirring frequently, for 10 minutes, or until they are soft but not brown. Stir in the chopped apple and cook for 2 or 3 minutes; then stir in the sauerkraut. Cover the casserole, reduce the heat as low as possible and braise the vegetables for 15 minutes. Then add the chicken stock, wine, and gin if it is being substituted for juniper berries. The stock should almost cover the sauerkraut; if it doesn't, add more stock. Season with salt and 4 or 5 grindings of pepper, and bury the *bouquet garni* in the sauerkraut. Bring the casserole to a boil on top of the stove; lay the salt pork on top. Cover the casserole tightly and place it on the middle shelf of the oven. After the sauerkraut has cooked for 3 hours, prick the sausage in 4 or 5 places and add it to the casserole. Cover and braise for another 30 minutes. Then spread the ham slices over the sauerkraut. Cover and braise for about 20 minutes longer, or until the ham is heated through.

To serve, discard the *bouquet garni*, transfer the sauerkraut to a deep, heated platter and mound the ham slices over it. Peel the sausage and cut it into 1-inch chunks; carve the salt pork into ⅛-inch slices. Arrange the sausage, salt pork and potatoes attractively around the sauerkraut.

Rôti de Porc Boulangère
GLAZED ROAST LOIN OF PORK

To serve 6

2 teaspoons salt
1 teaspoon coarsely ground black
  pepper
2 teaspoons finely cut fresh rosemary
  or 1½ teaspoons dried rosemary,
  crumbled
A 3-pound center-cut pork loin with
  the chine bone (backbone) sawed
  through but still attached, and
  circumference of loin tied in 2 or 3
  places
3 onions, coarsely chopped
2 carrots, cut in 1-inch chunks

Bouquet garni made of
  4 parsley sprigs and
  1 bay leaf, tied together
2 tablespoons butter
2 medium onions, thinly sliced
6 large firm boiling-type potatoes,
  cut in ¼-inch slices
Salt
Freshly ground black pepper
½ cup heated chicken stock, fresh
  or canned
1½ cups hot beef or chicken stock,
  fresh or canned, or a combination
  of both
2 tablespoons finely chopped fresh
  parsley

Preheat the oven to 475°. Combine the salt, pepper and rosemary, and press the mixture firmly into the pork roast. Place the seasoned pork, fat side up, in a heavy casserole just large enough to hold the pork. Roast uncovered on the middle shelf of the oven, turning the meat over 2 or 3 times, for 20 to 30 minutes, or until the pork is lightly browned. Then reduce the oven to 325°. Scatter the chopped onions, carrots and the *bouquet garni* around the pork, cover the casserole, and roast for 40 minutes longer, basting the pork every 10 minutes with the juices that accumulate in the pan.

Meanwhile butter the bottom and sides of a shallow baking-and-serving dish about 12 inches long and 1½ to 2 inches deep. Melt 2 tablespoons of butter in an 8- to 10-inch skillet, and in it cook the onions over moderate heat, stirring frequently, for 10 minutes, or until they are limp and lightly colored. When the pork is ready, spread the potato slices over the bottom of the baking dish and season with salt and pepper. Scatter the onions over the potato slices and pour in the heated stock. Place the pork loin on top and moisten both the pork and the potatoes with 2 or 3 tablespoons of fat skimmed from the drippings in the casserole. Roast uncovered in the bottom third of the oven for another 1¼ hours, or until the pork is crusty and glazed, and the potatoes and the onions are tender and brown.

While the pork is roasting, add 1½ cups of stock to the drippings left in the casserole. Bring to a boil over high heat and cook for 5 minutes, stirring frequently and scraping in any browned bits that cling to the bottom and sides of the pan. Strain the mixture through a fine sieve into a small saucepan, pressing down hard on the vegetables with the back of a spoon before discarding them. Let the liquid settle for a few minutes, then skim off the surface fat. Taste and season with salt and pepper. Set aside in the pan.

To serve, transfer the roast to a carving board, cut off the strings and slice the roast into 8 chops. Reheat the sauce made from the casserole drippings. Return the chops to the baking dish and arrange them in a line over the potatoes and onions. Moisten the pork with a little sauce and dust the potatoes with parsley. Serve the remaining sauce in a sauceboat.

Épaule d'Agneau Braisée aux Haricots
BRAISED SHOULDER OF LAMB WITH WHITE BEANS

To serve 6

4 tablespoons butter
3 onions, thinly sliced
3 carrots, cut in 1-inch chunks
A 7-pound shoulder of lamb, boned and tied (about 5 pounds boned)
1 or 2 garlic cloves, cut in ⅛-inch lengthwise slivers
¼ cup vegetable oil
1½ cups dry white wine
2 cups beef stock, fresh or canned
2 medium tomatoes, peeled, seeded and coarsely chopped
Bouquet garni made of 4 parsley sprigs, 1 leek (white part plus 2 inches of green) and 1 bay leaf, tied together
1 teaspoon dried thyme, crumbled
2½ teaspoons salt
Freshly ground black pepper
1½ quarts water
2 cups dry white beans (Great Northern, marrow, or navy)
2 tablespoons finely chopped fresh parsley

Preheat the oven to 350°. In a heavy flameproof casserole, just large enough to hold the lamb, and equipped with a cover, melt 4 tablespoons of butter over moderate heat. When the foam subsides, cook the onions and carrots, stirring occasionally, for 10 minutes, or until they are lightly colored. Meanwhile, make small incisions in the lamb and insert a sliver of garlic in each one. Heat the oil almost to the smoking point in a heavy 12- to 14-inch skillet and brown the lamb on all sides. Transfer the browned lamb to the casserole and place it, fat side up, on top of the vegetables.

Pour the wine into the skillet in which the lamb browned and boil it briskly, stirring and scraping in any bits that cling to the bottom and sides of the pan, until it has reduced to 1 cup. Add the beef stock, tomatoes, *bouquet garni*, thyme, ½ teaspoon of the salt and a few grindings of pepper, and return to a boil. Pour the stock over the lamb. Bring the casserole to a boil on top of the stove and drape a sheet of aluminum foil over the lamb. Cover the casserole tightly and cook in the lower third of the oven, regulating the heat so the lamb simmers slowly, for 3 hours

Continued on next page

or until the lamb is tender when pierced with the tip of a sharp knife.

While the lamb is braising, bring 1½ quarts of water to a bubbling boil in a heavy 4- to 6-quart saucepan or soup kettle. Drop the beans into the water and boil them briskly for 2 minutes. Remove the pan from the heat and let the beans soak for 1 hour. Return the pan to the heat, add the remaining 2 teaspoons salt and bring to a boil, then reduce the heat and simmer the beans, adding more water if necessary, for 1 to 1½ hours, or until they are just tender. Drain the beans and set aside.

When the lamb is done, transfer it to a plate and strain the rest of the contents of the casserole through a fine sieve into a mixing bowl; press down hard on the vegetables and herbs with the back of a spoon before discarding them. Skim as much fat as possible from the surface of the braising stock or sauce; taste and season it with salt and pepper if needed. Return the lamb and the beans to the casserole and pour the strained sauce over them. Heat the casserole on top of the stove until it comes to a simmer. To serve, carve the lamb into ¼-inch slices. Arrange the slices attractively on a heated platter, spoon a little stock over them and sprinkle them with parsley. Drain the beans and serve them from the same platter or a heated bowl; pass the remaining sauce separately in a sauceboat.

Pot-au-feu
BEEF SIMMERED WITH VEGETABLES

To serve 6

A 3-pound boneless beef rump, bottom round, brisket or chuck roast, tied
3 pounds beef marrow bones, sawed into 3-inch pieces
1 veal knuckle, sawed into pieces
1½ to 2 quarts beef stock, fresh or canned
2 tablespoons butter

2 whole onions, peeled
2 carrots, scraped and cut in half
1 medium tomato, peeled, seeded and coarsely chopped
Bouquet garni made of 4 parsley sprigs, 1 bay leaf and 1 leek (white part plus 2 inches of green), tied together
½ teaspoon dried thyme, crumbled
6 peppercorns
1 teaspoon salt

In a 6- to 8-quart saucepan or soup kettle, combine the beef, bones, knuckle and beef stock. The stock should rise about 4 inches above the meat; add more stock or water if needed. Bring to a boil over high heat. Meanwhile, melt the butter in a heavy 6- to 8-inch skillet, and cook the onions and carrots over moderate heat, turning them occasionally, until they are lightly colored. When the stock begins to boil, carefully skim all the foam and scum from the surface. Reduce the heat to low, skim the stock again and add the onions and carrots, chopped tomato, and the herbs and seasonings. Skim again. Partially cover the pot and simmer as slowly as possible, skimming when necessary, for 2½ hours, or until the meat is almost tender when pierced with the tip of a sharp knife. Transfer the meat to a plate, remove the bones from the stock and scoop out the marrow with the point of a knife before discarding them. Set the marrow aside in a bowl.

THE VEGETABLE GARNISH
6 carrots, peeled and cut in
   1½-inch-long cylinders or oval
   shapes
3 or 4 white turnips, peeled and
   quartered or cut in chunks
3 parsnips, peeled and quartered
6 leeks, white part plus 2 inches of
green, tied in a bundle (optional)
2 pounds cabbage, cored and cut in
   wedges (optional)
6 firm, boiling-type potatoes,
   unpeeled if new (optional)
8 tablespoons butter, melted
2 tablespoons finely chopped fresh
   parsley

Strain the stock through a fine sieve lined with a double layer of cheese-cloth into a large bowl. Discard the vegetables and skim the surface fat from the stock. Wash and dry the pot, then return the stock to it. Return the meat to the pot and add the garnish of carrots, turnips, parsnips and leeks. Bring the stock to a boil and cook uncovered over moderate heat for 30 minutes, or until the meat and vegetables are tender. If the vegetables cook faster than the meat, remove them from the pot and cook the meat until it is tender; then return the vegetables to the pot and heat them through. If you plan to serve cabbage with *pot-au-feu*, blanch it by plung-ing it into a kettle of boiling salted water and cooking it over high heat for 8 minutes. Drain the cabbage and add it to the meat and vegetables in the pot after they have cooked for 20 minutes.

If you plan to serve potatoes with the *pot-au-feu,* place them in a 2- to 3-quart saucepan, cover them with boiling water and cook them uncovered over moderately high heat for 20 to 30 minutes, or until tender. Drain the potatoes and keep them warm, but do not add them to the pot.

When the meat and vegetables are done, transfer the meat to a carving board, remove the strings and carve the roast into ¼-inch slices. Arrange the slices attractively, overlapping slightly, on a heated platter, surrounded by the vegetables and potatoes. Sprinkle melted butter over the vegetables and set aside. Chop the marrow into fine dice and add it to the stock in the pot. Serve the meat and vegetables and accompany them if you like with cup-fuls or a tureen of the cooking stock, first thoroughly degreased. Or you may serve the stock—sprinkled with a little chopped fresh parsley—as a first course.

Vegetables

Champignons à la Grecque
MARINATED MUSHROOMS

To serve 6

Marinade for *légumes à la grecque*
  (*page 8*)
1 pound fresh mushrooms, whole if
  small, quartered or sliced if large

Salt
Freshly ground black pepper
2 tablespoons finely chopped fresh
  parsley
2 lemons, cut in thin slices or quarters

In a 3- to 4-quart enameled or stainless-steel saucepan, prepare the marinade as described on page 8. After the marinade has been strained, return it to the saucepan and bring it to a simmer over moderate heat. Drop in the mushrooms, cover the pan and simmer for 10 minutes. With a slotted spoon, transfer the mushrooms to a stainless-steel or shallow glass baking dish. Taste the marinade for seasoning, then pour it over the mushrooms. Place the baking dish in the refrigerator to cool the mushrooms as quickly as possible. When they are chilled, cover the dish tightly with aluminum foil or plastic wrap and refrigerate for at least 4 hours before using. To serve, lift the mushrooms out of the marinade with a slotted spoon and arrange them attractively on a serving platter. Moisten the mushrooms with a little marinade, sprinkle them with parsley and garnish with lemon slices or quarters.

Poireaux Braisés
BRAISED LEEKS

To serve 6

12 firm fresh leeks, 1 to 1½ inches in
  diameter

2 cups beef stock, fresh or canned
4 tablespoons butter
Salt
Freshly ground black pepper

Cut off the roots of the leeks and strip away any withered leaves. Line up the leeks in a row and cut off enough green to make them all 6 or 7 inches long. Then with a sharp knife slit the green parts in half lengthwise, stopping where they shade into white. Carefully spread the leaves apart and wash them under fast-running water, looking out for any hidden pockets of sand. Lay the leeks in 1 or 2 layers in a heavy stainless-steel or enameled skillet or flameproof casserole just large enough to hold them flat. Pour in the beef stock and add the butter. Bring the stock to a boil over high heat; reduce the heat and boil gently, basting occasionally, for 15 minutes, or until the white parts of the leeks are tender when pierced with a sharp knife.

Preheat the oven to 325°. With tongs or a slotted spatula, arrange the leeks in one layer in a shallow, buttered baking dish. Taste the stock for seasoning, then pour it over the leeks and bake them covered loosely with a sheet of aluminum foil. In 20 minutes or so the leeks should be lightly colored and the stock almost cooked away. If the stock has not reduced enough, transfer it to a small saucepan with a bulb baster or spoon and boil it down. Serve the leeks directly from the baking dish or arrange them on a heated platter and pour the syrupy stock over them.

ALTERNATIVE: Celery may be braised in the same way. To serve 6, allow 6 small, whole bunches of stringless celery or 3 large bunches cut in half lengthwise.

Artichauts au Naturel
BOILED ARTICHOKES

To serve 6	1 lemon, cut
	6 quarts water
6 twelve- to fourteen-ounce artichokes	3 tablespoons salt

Trim the bases of the artichokes flush and flat. Bend and snap off the small bottom leaves and any bruised outer leaves. Lay each artichoke on its side, grip it firmly, and slice about 1 inch off the top. With scissors, trim ¼ inch off the points of the rest of the leaves. Rub all the cut edges with lemon to prevent discoloring. To remove the chokes before cooking, spread the top leaves apart and pull out the inner core of thistlelike yellow leaves. With a long-handled spoon, scrape out the hairy choke inside. Squeeze in a little lemon juice and press the artichoke back into shape.

In a large enameled kettle or soup pot, bring 6 quarts of water and 3 tablespoons of salt to a bubbling boil. Drop in the artichokes and return the water to a boil. Reduce the heat and boil briskly uncovered, turning the artichokes occasionally. It will take about 15 minutes to cook artichokes without their chokes, about 30 minutes with the chokes still in. They are done when their bases are tender when pierced with the tip of a sharp knife. Remove them from the kettle with tongs and drain them upside down in a colander. Serve the artichokes hot with melted butter, hollandaise (*page 13*) or béarnaise sauce (*page 14*). Or chill the artichokes and serve cold with vinaigrette (*page 16*) or mayonnaise (*page 13*).

Champignons Farcis

BAKED STUFFED MUSHROOM CAPS

To serve 6

MUSHROOMS WITH CRAB MEAT STUFFING

1½ cups lump crab meat, fresh, frozen
or canned

2 tablespoons butter

4 tablespoons finely chopped shallots
or scallions

1 cup *béchamel* sauce *(recipe opposite)*

¼ to ½ teaspoon lemon juice

Salt

White pepper

18 to 24 two-inch mushroom caps

CHAMPIGNONS FARCIS AU CRABE (mushrooms with crab meat stuffing): Preheat the oven to 350°. Carefully inspect the crab meat and remove any bits of cartilage, then shred the lumps with a fork. In a heavy 8- to 10-inch skillet, melt 2 tablespoons of butter over moderate heat and in it cook the shallots, stirring constantly, for 2 minutes, or until they are soft. Stir in the crab meat and toss it with the shallots for 10 seconds or so. With a rubber spatula, transfer the mixture to a large bowl.

Stir in the 1 cup *béchamel* sauce, then season to taste with lemon juice, salt and white pepper. Lightly butter a shallow baking dish or roasting pan large enough to hold the mushroom caps in one layer. Sprinkle the inside of the caps with salt, spoon in the crab filling and arrange the caps in the pan. Bake in the upper third of the oven for 10 to 15 minutes, or until the mushrooms are tender when pierced with the tip of a sharp knife and the filling is bubbly. Serve on a large heated platter.

MUSHROOMS WITH SPINACH STUFFING

½ cup finely chopped shallots or
scallions

3 tablespoons butter

¾ cup finely chopped, squeezed and
firmly packed cooked fresh spinach
(about ¾ pound) or 1 ten-ounce
package frozen, chopped spinach,

defrosted and squeezed dry

¾ cup finely chopped boiled ham

1 cup *béchamel* sauce *(recipe opposite)*

Salt

Freshly ground black pepper

18 to 24 two-inch mushroom caps

2 tablespoons butter, cut in tiny
pieces

CHAMPIGNONS FARCIS AUX ÉPINARDS (mushrooms with spinach and ham stuffing): Preheat the oven to 350°. In a heavy 8- to 10-inch skillet, cook the shallots in 3 tablespoons of butter over moderate heat, stirring constantly, for 2 minutes, or until soft. Add the spinach and toss it in the skillet for 3 to 4 minutes. With a rubber spatula, transfer the mixture to a large bowl. Stir in the ham and 1 cup *béchamel* sauce, and season with salt and pepper. Butter a large, shallow baking dish or roasting pan; sprinkle the caps with salt and spoon the filling into them. Arrange the caps in the pan and dot them with butter. Bake in the upper third of the oven for 10 to 15 minutes, or until the mushrooms are tender and the filling is lightly browned. Serve on a heated platter.

MUSHROOMS WITH MINCED
  MUSHROOM STUFFING
3/4 pound fresh mushrooms, finely
  chopped
4 tablespoons finely chopped shallots
  or scallions
2 tablespoons butter
1 cup *béchamel* sauce *(recipe below)*
1 teaspoon finely chopped fresh
parsley
Salt
Freshly ground black pepper
18 to 24 two-inch mushroom caps
2 tablespoons fine dry bread crumbs
1 tablespoon grated, imported Swiss
  cheese
2 tablespoons butter, cut in tiny pieces

CHAMPIGNONS FARCIS DUXELLES (mushrooms with minced mushroom stuffing): A handful at a time, squeeze the chopped mushrooms in the corner of a towel to extract as much juice as possible. Preheat the oven to 350°. In a heavy 8- to 10-inch skillet, cook the shallots in 2 tablespoons of butter over moderate heat, stirring constantly, for 2 minutes, or until they are soft. Add the chopped mushrooms and cook, stirring occasionally, for 8 to 10 minutes, or until all the moisture has evaporated and they are beginning to brown lightly. With a rubber spatula, transfer the mixture to a large bowl; stir in the 1 cup *béchamel* sauce and parsley, and season to taste with salt and pepper. Butter a large, shallow baking dish or roasting pan; salt the mushroom caps and spoon the filling into them. Mix the bread crumbs and grated cheese, then sprinkle them over the filling. Arrange the caps in the pan and dot them with butter. Bake in the upper third of the oven for 10 to 15 minutes, or until the mushrooms are tender and the filling is lightly browned. Serve hot or cold.

BÉCHAMEL SAUCE (Makes about 1 cup)
2 tablespoons butter
3 tablespoons flour
1 cup hot milk
Salt
White pepper

BÉCHAMEL SAUCE: In a heavy 2- to 3-quart saucepan, melt 2 tablespoons of butter over moderate heat, and stir in the flour. Cook, stirring constantly, for 2 minutes. Do not let this *roux* brown. Remove the pan from the heat and blend in the hot milk. Then return to high heat and cook, stirring constantly, until the sauce comes to a boil. Reduce the heat and simmer, still stirring, for 2 or 3 minutes, or until the sauce is thick enough to coat a spoon heavily. Remove the pan from the heat, taste and season with salt and white pepper.

Petits Pois Frais à la Française

FRESH PEAS BRAISED WITH ONIONS AND LETTUCE

To serve 4 to 6

	6 parsley sprigs, tied together
1 firm 7- to 8-inch head Boston lettuce	6 tablespoons butter, cut into ½-inch pieces
3 cups fresh shelled green peas (about 3 pounds)	½ cup water
	½ teaspoon salt
12 peeled white onions, about ¾ inch in diameter	½ teaspoon sugar
	2 tablespoons soft butter

Remove the wilted outer leaves of the lettuce and trim the stem. Rinse the lettuce in cold water, spreading the leaves apart gently, to remove all traces of sand. Cut the lettuce into 4 or 6 wedges, and bind each wedge with soft string to keep it in shape while cooking.

In a heavy 3-quart saucepan, bring the peas, lettuce wedges, onions, parsley, 6 tablespoons butter, water, salt and sugar to a boil over moderate heat, toss lightly to mix flavors, then cover the pan tightly and cook for 30 minutes, stirring occasionally, until the peas and onions are tender and the liquid nearly cooked away. If the liquid hasn't evaporated, cook the peas uncovered, shaking the pan constantly, for a minute or two until it does. Remove the parsley and cut the strings off the lettuce. Gently stir in 2 tablespoons of soft butter; taste and season. Transfer to a heated vegetable dish and serve in small bowls. It is traditional to eat *petits pois* with a spoon.

Champignons Grillés

BROILED MUSHROOMS

Fresh mushroom caps of the size and in the quantity desired	Freshly ground black pepper
Melted butter	Small toast rounds (optional)
	Soft butter
Salt	Lemon juice

Preheat the broiler. Using a pastry brush, paint each mushroom cap with melted butter. Arrange the caps side by side and hollow side up in a well-buttered, shallow baking dish. Season them lightly with salt and pepper and broil them 6 inches from the heat for 5 minutes. Gently turn the caps over and broil them for another 5 minutes, or until they are lightly browned and tender when pierced with the tip of a sharp knife.

To serve, arrange them on a heated platter (on toast rounds if desired). Dot the tops with a bit of soft butter and sprinkle each cap with a few drops of lemon juice.

Haricots Verts au Naturel

GREEN STRING BEANS, BLANCHED AND BUTTERED

To serve 6 to 8

6 quarts water
3 tablespoons salt

3 pounds green string beans, trimmed
2 tablespoons butter
Salt
Freshly ground black pepper

In a large kettle or soup pot, bring the water and 3 tablespoons of salt to a bubbling boil over high heat. Drop the beans in by the handful. Return the water to a boil, reduce the heat to moderate and boil the beans uncovered for 10 to 15 minutes, or until they are just tender. Do not overcook them. Immediately drain them in a large sieve or colander. If the beans are to be served at once, melt 2 tablespoons of butter in a 2- to 3-quart saucepan and toss the beans with the butter for a minute or two, season them with salt and pepper, then transfer them to a serving dish.

If the beans are to be served later, refresh them after they have drained by quickly plunging the sieve or colander into a large pot of cold water and letting it remain there for 2 or 3 minutes. Drain the beans thoroughly, place them in a bowl, cover and set aside—in the refrigerator if they are to wait for long. If you plan to serve them hot, reheat them in 2 tablespoons of hot butter, season them and let them warm through over moderate heat.

Chou Rouge à la Limousine

BRAISED RED CABBAGE IN RED WINE WITH CHESTNUTS

To serve 6

¼ pound salt pork, diced
2 cups water
½ cup finely chopped onions
3 pounds red cabbage cut into julienne
    strips (about 12 cups)
1½ cups dry red wine
1½ cups beef stock, fresh or canned

2 tablespoons wine vinegar
⅛ teaspoon ground nutmeg
⅛ teaspoon ground cloves
1 teaspoon salt
Freshly ground black pepper
1 two-pound can whole unflavored
    chestnuts (not marrons glacés),
    drained and washed

Preheat the oven to 325°. Blanch the salt pork by simmering it in 2 cups of water for 5 minutes. Drain the salt pork and dry it with paper towels. In a heavy 4- to 5-quart flameproof casserole that has a tight fitting cover, cook the pork over moderate heat, stirring frequently, until the dice are crisp and golden and have rendered all their fat. With a slotted spoon, remove the pork dice and reserve them. Cook the onions in the fat remaining in the casserole over moderate heat, stirring frequently, for 5 minutes, or until

Continued on next page

soft but not brown. Stir in the cabbage, cover the casserole and cook over low heat for 10 minutes.

Add the wine, beef stock, vinegar, nutmeg, cloves, salt pork dice, salt and a generous grinding of pepper to the cabbage. Cover the casserole again and bake on the middle shelf of the oven for 2 hours. (Check to be sure the liquids are not cooking away too fast; if they seem to be, add more stock.) Gently stir in the chestnuts and bake covered for 1 hour more, or until the cabbage is tender and most of the liquid has been absorbed. Correct seasoning and serve from the casserole or a heated vegetable dish.

Pommes de Terre Dauphinoises
SCALLOPED POTATOES WITH CHEESE

To serve 6

1 garlic clove, peeled and bruised
   with the flat of a knife
2½ pounds firm boiling potatoes,
   old or new, peeled and cut into
   ⅛-inch slices (about 8 cups)

1½ cups grated, imported Swiss cheese
6 tablespoons butter, cut in ¼-inch
   bits
1 teaspoon salt
⅛ teaspoon coarsely ground black
   pepper
1¼ cups milk

Preheat the oven to 425°. Rub the bottom and sides of a flameproof baking-and-serving dish, 10 to 12 inches across and 2 inches deep, with the bruised garlic, and grease it lightly with butter. Dry the potato slices with a paper towel, then spread half of the slices in the bottom of the dish. Sprinkle them with half the cheese, butter bits, salt and pepper. Spread the rest of the slices in the dish and sprinkle the remaining cheese, butter, salt and pepper on top. Pour the milk into the side of the dish. Bring to a simmer over low heat and then bake in the upper third of the oven for 20 minutes, or until the potatoes are almost tender when pierced with the tip of a sharp knife. At this point remove any residual liquid with a bulb baster and bake for another 5 minutes, or until the potatoes are tender, the milk absorbed, and the top nicely browned. Serve at once.

Asperges au Naturel
BOILED ASPARAGUS
To serve 6

3 pounds fresh asparagus

6 quarts water
3 tablespoons salt

Line up the asparagus tips evenly and cut off the butt ends to make all the spears the same length. With a small, sharp knife, *not* a vegetable peeler, peel each asparagus of its skin and tough outer flesh. At the butt end, the peeling may be as thick as 1/16 inch, but it should gradually become paper thin as the knife cuts and slides toward the tip. Wash the peeled spears in cold water. Divide the asparagus into five or six equal bundles, and tie the bundles together with soft string at both the tip and butt ends.

In an enameled or stainless steel kettle or oval casserole large enough to hold the asparagus horizontally, bring the water and salt to a bubbling boil. Drop in the asparagus bundles and bring the water back to a boil. Reduce the heat to moderate and boil uncovered for 8 to 10 minutes, or until the butt ends are tender but still slightly resistant when pierced with the tip of a sharp knife. Do not overcook the asparagus. Using two kitchen forks, lift the bundles out of the water by their strings. Lay them on towels to drain, then cut off the strings. Serve the asparagus hot with melted butter or hollandaise sauce *(page 13)*. Or chill and serve cold with vinaigrette sauce *(page 16)* or mayonnaise *(page 13)*.

Tomates à la Provençale
TOMATOES BAKED WITH BREAD CRUMBS AND GARLIC

To serve 6	1/2 cup finely chopped fresh parsley
	1 tablespoon finely cut fresh basil or
6 firm ripe tomatoes, 3 to 4 inches	2 teaspoons dried basil, crumbled
in diameter	1 large garlic clove, finely chopped
Salt	1 teaspoon salt
1 cup dry white homemade bread	Freshly ground black pepper
crumbs, not too fine in texture	1/3 to 1/2 cup olive oil

Cut the tomatoes in half crosswise. With a finger or the handle of a teaspoon, scoop out the seeds. Sprinkle the inside of the tomatoes with salt and turn them upside down to drain on paper towels. Preheat the oven to 375°.

In a large mixing bowl, stir together the bread crumbs, parsley, basil, garlic, 1 teaspoon salt and a few grindings of pepper. Add enough olive oil to moisten the stuffing but still leave it crumbly. Fill each tomato half with about 2 tablespoons of the crumb mixture, patting it in and letting it mound up a little in the middle. Arrange the tomato halves in one or two lightly oiled shallow baking dishes; do not crowd them. Sprinkle a few drops of oil over each half. Bake in the upper third of the oven for 20 to 30 minutes, or until the tomatoes are tender but not limp. With a wide metal spatula, transfer the tomatoes to a heated platter and serve them hot. Or chill the tomatoes and serve them cold, sprinkled with chopped parsley.

Carottes Glacées
GLAZED CARROTS

To serve 4 to 6

10 to 12 medium carrots, peeled and
    cut in 2-inch cylinders or olive
    shapes
1½ cups beef or chicken stock, fresh
    or canned

4 tablespoons butter
2 tablespoons sugar
½ teaspoon salt
Freshly ground black pepper
2 tablespoons finely chopped, fresh
    parsley

In a heavy 8- to 10-inch skillet, bring the carrots, stock, butter, sugar, salt
and a few grindings of pepper to a boil over moderate heat. Then cover and
simmer over low heat, shaking the skillet occasionally to roll the carrots
about in the liquid. Check to see that the liquid is not cooking away too
fast; if it is, add more stock. In 20 to 30 minutes the carrots should be
tender when pierced with the tip of a sharp knife, and the braising liquid
should be a brown, syrupy glaze. If the stock has not reduced enough, remove the carrots to a plate and boil the liquid down over high heat. Before
serving, roll the carrots around in the pan to coat them with the glaze.
Transfer the carrots to a heated vegetable dish, and sprinkle them with fresh
parsley.

NOTE: This technique may also be used for parsnips and for white and
yellow turnips.

Oignons Glacés à Blanc
GLAZED WHITE ONIONS

To serve 4 to 6

⅔ cup chicken stock, fresh or canned
2 tablespoons butter

Salt
Freshly ground black pepper
16 to 24 peeled white onions, about
    1 inch in diameter

In a heavy 8- to 10-inch skillet, bring the chicken stock, butter, and salt and
pepper to taste to a boil. Drop in the onions, reduce the heat, cover and
simmer very slowly for 20 to 30 minutes, or until the onions are tender,
turning the onions occasionally with a spoon. The braising liquid should
have reduced to a syrupy glaze; if it hasn't, remove the onions and boil the
liquid down alone. Roll the onions around gently in the pan to moisten
them with glaze before serving them in a heated vegetable dish.

Pommes de Terre Anna
CRUSTY MOLDED POTATOES

To serve 4 to 6

8 tablespoons butter
2½ pounds mealy-textured baking
   potatoes, peeled

Salt
Freshly ground black pepper
1 tablespoon finely chopped fresh
   parsley

First, clarify the butter in a small, heavy saucepan or skillet by melting it slowly, skimming off the surface foam. Spoon the clear butter on top into a bowl and discard the milky solids (whey) at the bottom of the pan. There should be about 6 tablespoons of clarified butter.

With a vegetable slicer or thin sharp knife, carefully cut the potatoes into slices no more than 1/16-inch thick. Do not soak, rinse or dry the slices. In a heavy 8-inch skillet with sloping sides, heat 2 tablespoons of clarified butter, swirling it around to coat the bottom and sides of the pan evenly, until it is hot but not sizzling. Remove the skillet from the heat, lay potato slices in concentric circles, with each slice slightly overlapping the last, over the bottom of the skillet. With a pastry brush, spread a little more butter on top of the slices; season them lightly with salt and pepper. Then shake the skillet back and forth to be sure the potato slices move together as one mass without sticking to the bottom of the pan. If they don't slide freely, loosen the bottom with a metal spatula and cook them over low heat for 10 seconds to heat the butter and set the potatoes.

Off the heat, arrange a second layer of potatoes in concentric circles, brush with butter, season with salt and pepper, and shake the pan again to be sure the bottom layer is still free. Continue to build up layers of potatoes, buttering and seasoning each one, until the skillet is full. Pour the remaining butter over the top layer of potatoes.

Return the skillet to moderate heat and cook, shaking gently and constantly, to keep the potatoes moving as one mass, until the butter sizzles. Reduce the heat to low, cover the pan tightly, and cook—gently shaking the pan from time to time—for 30 minutes, or until the upper layers of potatoes are tender when pierced with the point of a sharp knife.

When the potatoes are done, remove the cover and slide a narrow metal spatula around the inside edge of the skillet, freeing any potatoes that stick to the sides. Gently force the spatula down and as far under the potatoes as possible without disrupting the design. Place a round heated platter upside down over the skillet and, grasping the platter and skillet together, reverse them quickly. The potatoes should emerge as a round, compact cake. If any slices stick to the skillet, carefully lift them out and put them where they belong on the cake. Before serving, remove any butter that collects on the platter with a basting syringe. Garnish the potatoes with chopped parsley.

Ratatouille

MEDITERRANEAN VEGETABLE CASSEROLE

To serve 6 to 8

3 pounds firm ripe tomatoes

1½ to 2 pounds eggplant, peeled and
   sliced ¾ inch thick

1½ pounds zucchini, unpeeled, sliced
   ½ inch thick

¼ to ½ cup olive oil

¾ pound green peppers, seeded and

cut in 1-inch squares (about 2 cups)

2½ cups thinly sliced onions

½ cup finely chopped fresh parsley

1 tablespoon finely cut fresh basil or
   2 teaspoons dried basil, crumbled

2 teaspoons finely chopped garlic
   cloves

Salt

Freshly ground black pepper

Peel the tomatoes, cut them into quarters, and cut away the pulp and seeds, leaving only the shells. Cut the shells into ½-inch-wide strips and drain on paper towels. Lightly salt the eggplant and zucchini slices, spread them in one layer between paper towels, and weight them with a large, heavy platter. After 20 to 30 minutes, dry the eggplant and zucchini thoroughly with fresh paper towels.

In a heavy 10- to 12-inch skillet, bring ¼ cup of olive oil almost to the smoking point over moderately high heat, and brown the eggplant slices for a minute or two on each side, working quickly to prevent them from soaking up too much oil. Don't worry if they don't brown evenly. Remove them to paper towels to drain. In the same skillet, lightly brown the zucchini, peppers and onions one after another, adding more oil whenever necessary. Drain the zucchini and peppers on paper towels, but remove the onions to a plate. With a fork, stir the parsley, basil and garlic together in a small bowl.

Pour 1 tablespoon of the oil remaining in the skillet into a heavy 4- to 5-quart enameled casserole. Spread one third of the eggplant slices on the bottom, sprinkle with 1 teaspoon of the herb and garlic mixture, and season with salt and pepper. Arrange successive layers of half the zucchini, half the peppers, half the onions and half the tomatoes—sprinkling herbs and salt and pepper on each layer. Repeat. Finish with a layer of the remaining eggplant. Sprinkle with the remaining parsley mixture, salt and pepper, and pour in the oil left in the skillet.

Over moderately high heat, bring the casserole to a boil, cover and reduce the heat to a simmer. Every 7 or 8 minutes, use a bulb baster to draw up the liquid that will accumulate in the casserole. Transfer the liquid to a small saucepan. In 20 to 30 minutes, when the vegetables are tender but still somewhat firm, remove the casserole from the heat. Briskly boil the liquid in the saucepan for a few minutes to reduce it to about 2 tablespoons of glaze, and pour it into the casserole. Serve the *ratatouille* directly from the casserole, either hot or cold.

Laitues Braisées

BRAISED LETTUCE

To serve 6

6 firm 6-inch heads Boston lettuce
7 quarts water
Salt
Freshly ground black pepper
6 bacon slices, cut ¼ inch thick
1 four-inch square of bacon rind
  (optional)
2 tablespoons butter

½ cup thinly sliced onions
½ cup thinly sliced carrots
1 cup beef or chicken stock, fresh or
  canned
6 parsley sprigs
1 bay leaf
2 tablespoons soft butter
2 tablespoons finely chopped fresh
  parsley

Remove the wilted outer leaves and trim the stems of the lettuce. Rinse the heads in cold water, spreading the leaves apart gently, to remove all traces of sand. Bring 6 quarts of water and 3 tablespoons of salt to a bubbling boil in a large kettle or soup pot. Drop the lettuce in and blanch it, uncovered, for 3 to 5 minutes, or until the outer leaves are limp. Immediately remove the lettuce with tongs and plunge it into cold water for 2 or 3 minutes. Then, gently squeeze each head dry and slice it in half lengthwise. (Do not be concerned if the inner leaves have turned somewhat brown.) Season both halves with salt and a few grindings of pepper, and fold and shape them into small cushions. Set aside on paper towels.

Preheat the oven to 325°. Blanch the bacon slices and optional rind by simmering them in 1 quart of boiling water for 5 minutes; drain. In a flameproof 12-inch casserole that has a cover, melt 2 tablespoons of butter over moderate heat. When the foam subsides, stir in the onions and carrots, and cook them, stirring occasionally, for 5 minutes, or until they are tender but not brown. Remove the casserole from the heat, arrange the lettuce on top of the onions and carrots, and drape the bacon and rind over it. Pour in the stock and add the parsley sprigs and bay leaf. Bring to a simmer on top of the stove, cover tightly and bake in the lower third of the oven for 1½ hours. To serve, arrange the lettuce attractively on a heated platter with the bacon slices around it. Remove and discard the rind and bay leaf. Boil down the braising liquid briskly over high heat until it has reduced to about ½ cup. Remove the casserole from the heat, swirl in 2 tablespoons of soft butter and strain the sauce over the lettuce. Sprinkle with parsley and serve at once.

Desserts

Tartes aux Fraises

FRESH STRAWBERRY TARTS

To serve 6

	3 tablespoons flour
6 individual 3- to 4-inch *pâte brisée* tart shells or 9- to 10-inch *pâte brisée* shell (*page 4*)	Pinch of salt
	1 envelope unflavored gelatin
	1 teaspoon vanilla extract
1 egg plus 1 extra egg yolk	1 cup hot milk
¼ cup sugar	1 cup heavy cream

Preheat the oven to 400° and bake the pastry shells (or shell) as described in the recipe for *pâte brisée*, adding another 7 to 10 minutes to the final baking to brown the shell lightly and cook it fully. Unmold the shells (or shell) and slip it onto a wire cake rack to cool.

In a heavy 2- to 3-quart saucepan—off the heat—beat the egg, the extra egg yolk and the sugar with a wire whisk, rotary or electric beater until the mixture thickens and turns a pale yellow. Add the flour and salt, and beat until well blended. Beat in the powdered gelatin and vanilla; then slowly pour in the hot milk in a thin stream, beating constantly. Cook over moderate heat, stirring with a whisk, until smooth and thick. Do not allow the custard to boil; if it seems to be getting too hot, lift the pan off the heat a few seconds to cool it. If the custard gets lumpy, beat it with a whisk or rotary beater until smooth. Pour the custard into a large mixing bowl and place in the refrigerator to cool. When the custard is cold and has begun to solidify slightly, whip the cream until it holds soft peaks. Fold it thoroughly into the custard with a rubber spatula and beat gently if there are any lumps. At once, pour or spoon the custard into the pastry shells.

CURRANT GLAZE

1 cup red currant jelly	1 to 1½ quarts large ripe
1 tablespoon hot water	strawberries, cleaned and stemmed
1 tablespoon kirsch	Confectioners' (powdered) sugar

CURRANT GLAZE: In a small saucepan, warm the red currant jelly and hot water over low heat, stirring occasionally, until they begin to froth and thicken. Remove the saucepan from the heat, stir in the kirsch and let the glaze cool a bit.

Meanwhile, arrange the strawberries on the custard, stem side down—and in concentric circles if the tart is a large one—until the top of each tart is completely covered with berries. Spoon the warm glaze over the berries. Refrigerate the tarts for at least 2 hours, or until the custard is firm. Sprinkle them with confectioners' sugar before serving.

Paris-Brest

CREAM-PUFF PASTRY RING WITH WHIPPED CREAM FILLING

To serve 6

	almonds
PÂTE À CHOUX *(page 98)*	2 cups heavy cream
1 egg	1 tablespoon confectioners'
½ teaspoon water	(powdered) sugar
3 tablespoons blanched, slivered	2 teaspoons vanilla extract

Preheat the oven to 450°. Butter a baking sheet, scatter a little flour over it, and tap the edge on the table to knock off the excess flour. Then lay an 8-inch plate or pan on the sheet, pressing down hard to make a circular impression in the flour. Remove the plate or pan. Using a pastry tube with a large plain tip, make a circle or crown of *pâte à choux* 2 inches wide and 1 inch high around the pattern in the flour. If you don't have a pastry tube, drop the paste by spoonfuls, placing the mounds side by side around the ring, then, with a spatula, smooth the mounds into a continuous strand, 2 inches wide and 1 inch high. Beat the egg and water together and paint the top of the crown with the mixture. Sprinkle it with slivered almonds. Bake on the middle shelf of the oven 10 minutes, then reduce the heat to 350° and bake 10 minutes more. Reduce the heat to 325° and bake for 20 minutes, or until the crown has more than doubled in size and is golden brown, firm and crusty. Turn off the oven and make 3 or 4 tiny cuts near the bottom of the crown with the tip of a sharp knife. Let the crown rest in the oven for 5 minutes to dry out. Slice it in half horizontally with a serrated knife, and spoon out any soft dough inside the shells.

No more than 1 hour before serving, whip the cream with a wire whisk, rotary or electric beater in a large chilled mixing bowl until it begins to thicken. Add the sugar and vanilla, and continue beating until the cream holds its shape firmly. Using a pastry bag with a decorative tip, or a tablespoon, fill the bottom part of the crown with whipped cream. The cream should rise well above the rim of the pastry. Gently replace the top of the crown so that it floats on the cream. Sprinkle the top with confectioners' sugar and refrigerate the *Paris-Brest* until serving time.

Profiteroles

CREAM-PUFF PASTRY ROSETTES

To serve 8 to 10

PÂTE À CHOUX, OR CREAM-PUFF PASTE
1 cup water
6 tablespoons butter, cut into small
   pieces

1 cup all-purpose flour, sifted after
   measuring
1 teaspoon sugar
5 eggs (U.S. graded ''large'')
½ teaspoon water

PÂTE À CHOUX: In a heavy 2- to 3-quart saucepan, bring the 1 cup of water and the butter to a boil over moderate heat, stirring occasionally. As
soon as the butter has completely melted, remove the pan from the heat
and pour in the flour and sugar all at once. Beat the mixture vigorously
with a wooden spoon for a few seconds until it is well blended. Then return it to moderate heat and cook, still beating vigorously, for 1 or 2
minutes, or until the mixture forms a mass that leaves the sides of the pan
and moves freely with the spoon.

Immediately remove the pan from the heat and use the spoon to make a
well in the center of the paste. Break an egg into the well and beat it into
the paste. When the first egg has been absorbed, add 3 more eggs 1 at a
time—beating well after each egg is added. The finished paste should be
thick, smooth and shiny.

Preheat the oven to 425°. Lightly butter two large baking sheets. Spoon
the *pâte à choux* into a pastry bag that has a ¼- or ½-inch plain tip, and press
the paste out onto the sheets in mounds, about 1 inch in diameter and ½
inch high. Space the mounds approximately 2 inches apart; they will double
in size as they bake. If you don't have a pastry bag, drop teaspoonfuls of
the paste onto the baking sheets, allowing the same 2 inches of space
between them.

Beat the remaining egg with ½ teaspoon of water in a small bowl until
they are well mixed. With a pastry brush, lightly paint the top of each *profiterole* with the egg-and-water mixture. Bake in the upper and/or lower third
of the oven for 6 minutes, then reduce the heat to 400° and bake for 5
minutes longer.

Reduce the heat to 325° and bake for another 15 to 20 minutes, or until
the *profiteroles* have doubled in size and have turned a light golden brown.
They should be firm and crusty to the touch. Turn off the oven and make
a tiny incision near the bottom of each *profiterole* with the tip of a sharp
knife to release the steam. Let the *profiteroles* rest in the oven for a few
minutes to dry out. Then remove them from the baking sheets and set
them on wire cake racks to cool.

FILLING	CHOCOLATE SAUCE
1 cup heavy cream	8 ounces semisweet chocolate, cut
3 tablespoons confectioners'	into small chunks
(powdered) sugar	½ cup strong coffee
1 tablespoon vanilla extract	Confectioners' (powdered) sugar

FILLING AND CHOCOLATE SAUCE: No more than 1 hour before serving the *profiteroles*, whip the cream with a wire whisk, rotary or electric beater in a chilled mixing bowl until it begins to thicken. Sprinkle the confectioners' sugar and the vanilla over it, and continue beating until the cream is firm enough to hold unwavering peaks on the beater when the beater is raised out of the bowl.

Gently break the top off each *profiterole* or slit it in half with a small, sharp knife. Fill the bottom half with a spoonful of heavy cream, replace the top and gently press the *profiterole* together again. Dust the top lightly with confectioners' sugar. Melt the chocolate with the coffee in a small, heavy saucepan over hot water, stirring constantly until the mixture is perfectly smooth.

To serve, pour a little of the warm chocolate sauce into individual dessert dishes and float two or more of the *profiteroles* on top. Or, if you prefer, you may serve the *profiteroles* on dessert plates with the chocolate sauce poured over them.

Compote de Fruits
FRUIT POACHED IN VANILLA SYRUP

To serve 4

	1½ tablespoons vanilla extract
3 cups water	4 ripe but firm pears or peaches or 8
1 cup sugar	apricots, peeled, halved and cored
1 two-inch piece of vanilla bean or	or stoned

In a 12-inch enameled saucepan, bring the water, sugar and vanilla to a boil over moderate heat, stirring until the sugar dissolves. Add the fruit, reduce the heat, and cook uncovered at a very slow simmer for 15 to 20 minutes, or until the fruit is soft but not mushy when pierced with the tip of a sharp knife. Let the fruit cool in the syrup for 30 minutes. With a slotted spoon, transfer the fruit to a serving bowl or baking dish. Boil the syrup briskly over high heat until it thickens slightly, and pour it over the fruit. Refrigerate the fruit, and serve it chilled in dessert dishes, small bowls or champagne glasses with a spoonful of syrup to moisten each of the portions.

Diplomate

MOLDED CUSTARD WITH GLACÉED FRUITS

To serve 10 to 12

½ cup kirsch
½ cup diced mixed candied fruit
2 dozen best quality (or home-made
    type) ladyfingers, split in half
1 envelope plus 1 extra teaspoon

unflavored gelatin
⅓ cup water
1 cup milk
5 egg yolks
¼ cup sugar
1½ cups chilled heavy cream
½ cup apricot preserves

In a small bowl, combine ¼ cup of the kirsch with the diced candied fruit, and set them aside at room temperature to steep. Lay a circle of wax paper on the bottom of a 2-quart charlotte mold or any other plain, round 2-quart mold 3 or 4 inches deep. Line the mold with ladyfingers by first cutting a ½-inch circle out of a ladyfinger half and placing it, curved side down, in the center of the paper. (Save the scraps to use later.) Then cut ladyfingers into slightly tapered wedge shapes to fit and radiate around the circle—like petals in a rosette—and arrange them, curved side down, on the paper. Stand more ladyfingers side by side around the inside of the mold, trimming off any excess above the rim. Set the mold and the rest of the ladyfingers aside.

    In a heatproof measuring cup or small bowl, sprinkle the gelatin over ¼ cup of water. When the gelatin has softened for 2 or 3 minutes, set the cup in a small skillet of simmering water and cook over low heat, stirring constantly, until the gelatin dissolves. Remove the skillet from the heat, but leave the cup of gelatin in the skillet to keep warm.

    In a heavy 2- to 3-quart saucepan, heat the milk until bubbles begin to form around the edge of the pan; remove from the stove. With a whisk, rotary or electric beater, beat the egg yolks and sugar together in a bowl for 3 or 4 minutes, or until the yolks are pale yellow and slightly thickened. Stirring continually, pour the hot milk in a thin stream over the egg yolks. When thoroughly blended, pour into a clean saucepan. Stirring constantly, cook over low heat until the custard begins to thicken; continue cooking, stirring constantly, until the custard coats the spoon like heavy cream. Do not let the custard come near the boil or it will curdle; if it gets too hot, lift the pan off the stove to cool it.

    Then remove the pan from the heat and stir in the dissolved gelatin, blending it through the custard completely. Strain the custard through a fine sieve into a large mixing bowl. With a wire whisk, rotary or electric beater, whip the cream in a large chilled mixing bowl until it forms soft peaks. Set the bowl of custard into a large pot filled with crushed ice or ice cubes and water. Stir the custard for 4 or 5 minutes or until it is quite cold and begins to thicken. Beat thoroughly with a wire whisk to be sure it is perfectly smooth. Then scoop the whipped cream over the custard and use a rubber spatula to fold them together gently but thoroughly. If there are any lumps, beat gently with a whisk or rotary beater until smooth. Fold in the candied fruit and kirsch.

Force the apricot preserves through a fine sieve into a small saucepan. Stir in the remaining ¼ cup kirsch and bring to a boil over moderate heat, stirring constantly. Brush the ladyfingers lining the mold lightly with the hot apricot glaze. Ladle half of the custard into the mold, then arrange ladyfingers in a neat but informal layer on the custard. Ladle in the rest of the custard and cover the top with whatever ladyfingers are left; even the scraps will do. Chill for 4 or 5 hours, or until firm and set.

To unmold and serve the *diplomate,* run a sharp knife around the sides of the mold and dip the bottom in hot water for a few seconds. Then wipe the outside of the mold dry, place a chilled serving plate upside down over the mold and, grasping both sides firmly, turn the plate and mold over. Rap the plate on a table and the *diplomate* should slide out of the mold. If it doesn't unmold at once, repeat the whole process. Gently remove the wax paper from the top, and chill the *diplomate* again before serving.

Poires Pochées au Vin Rouge
PEARS POACHED IN RED WINE

To serve 6

2 cups dry red wine
2 tablespoons lemon juice
1 cup sugar

1 two-inch stick of cinnamon or ½ teaspoon ground cinnamon
6 small or 3 large ripe but firm pears, peeled, cored and halved

In a 12-inch enameled saucepan, bring the wine, lemon juice, sugar and cinnamon to a boil over moderate heat, stirring until the sugar dissolves. Add the pear halves, partially cover the pan and reduce the heat to low. Cook the pears at a very slow simmer for 15 to 20 minutes, or until they are soft but not mushy when pierced with the tip of a sharp knife. Cool the pears in the syrup until they are lukewarm. If you would like to serve the pear halves warm, discard the cinnamon stick and use a slotted spoon to transfer the pears to dessert dishes, small bowls or champagne glasses. Spoon a bit of the syrup over them. To serve the pears cold, refrigerate them in the syrup in a large bowl or baking dish until they are thoroughly chilled.

Crème Caramel

CARAMEL CUSTARD

To serve 6

CARAMEL
½ cup sugar
¼ cup water
Pinch of cream of tartar

CUSTARD
2 cups milk
1 teaspoon vanilla extract or 1 three-
   inch piece of vanilla bean
¼ cup sugar
3 eggs plus 2 extra egg yolks

To line a 1-quart metal or porcelain mold or six 4-ounce heatproof porcelain or glass individual molds with caramel, it is necessary to work quickly. Remember in handling the caramel that it will be over 300°, so be extremely careful with it. Place the mold (or molds) on a large strip of wax paper. Then, in a small, heavy saucepan or skillet, bring the sugar and water to a boil over high heat, stirring until the sugar dissolves. Stir in a pinch of cream of tartar and—gripping a pot holder in each hand—boil the syrup over moderate heat, gently tipping the pan back and forth almost constantly, until the syrup turns a rich, golden, tea-like brown. This may take 10 minutes or more. As soon as the syrup reaches the right color, remove the pan from the heat and carefully pour the caramel syrup in a thin stream into the mold (or the first of the individual molds). Still using the pot holders, tip and swirl the mold to coat the bottom and sides as evenly as possible. When the syrup stops moving, turn the mold upside down on the wax paper to cool somewhat and to let any excess syrup run out.

Preheat oven to 325°. In a 1- to 1½-quart saucepan, bring the milk almost to a boil over moderate heat. Remove the pan from the stove and add the vanilla extract. With a wire whisk, rotary or electric beater, beat the sugar, eggs and extra egg yolks until they are well mixed and thickened. Stirring gently and constantly, pour in the milk in a thin stream. Strain through a fine sieve into the caramel-lined mold and place the mold (or molds) in a large pan on the middle shelf of the oven. Pour enough boiling water into the pan to come halfway up the sides of the mold. Bake the custard—lowering the oven temperature if the water in the pan begins to simmer—for about 1 hour, or until a knife inserted in the center of the custard comes out clean. Remove the mold from the water and refrigerate the custard for at least 3 hours, or until it is thoroughly chilled.

To unmold and serve the large custard, run a sharp knife around the sides and dip the bottom of the mold briefly in hot water. Then wipe the outside of the mold dry, place a chilled serving plate upside down over the mold and, grasping both sides firmly, quickly turn the plate and mold over. Rap the plate on a table and the custard should slide easily out of the mold. Unmold the individual custards carefully, turning them out one at a time on individual serving plates. Pour any extra caramel remaining in the mold (or molds) over the custard. Serve cold.

Pêches Cardinal
POACHED PEACHES WITH RASPBERRY PURÉE

To serve 8	8 large ripe but firm peaches, peeled, halved and stoned
6 cups water	1 four-inch piece of vanilla bean or
2 cups sugar	3 tablespoons vanilla extract

In a heavy 3- to 4-quart saucepan, bring the water and sugar to a boil over high heat, stirring until the sugar dissolves. Boil this syrup briskly for 3 minutes, then reduce the heat as low as possible. Add the peeled peach halves and vanilla and poach them uncovered at a very low simmer for 10 to 20 minutes, or until they are barely tender when pierced with the tip of a sharp knife. Refrigerate the peaches in the syrup until they are cold.

SAUCE CARDINAL

| 2 ten-ounce packages frozen raspberries, defrosted and thoroughly drained | 2 tablespoons superfine sugar |
| | 1 tablespoon kirsch |

SAUCE CARDINAL: With the back of a large spoon, purée the raspberries through a fine sieve into a small mixing bowl. Stir 2 tablespoons of superfine sugar and the kirsch into the raspberry purée. Refrigerate, tightly covered.

CRÈME CHANTILLY

¾ cup heavy cream, thoroughly chilled	
2 tablespoons superfine sugar	GARNISH
1 tablespoon vanilla extract	Whole fresh raspberries or defrosted frozen raspberries (optional)

CRÈME CHANTILLY: With a wire whisk, rotary or electric beater, whip the cream in a chilled mixing bowl until it begins to thicken. Sprinkle in 2 table-spoons of superfine sugar and the vanilla; continue beating until the cream is firm enough to hold soft peaks on the beater when it is raised out of the bowl.

To serve, transfer the chilled peach halves with a slotted spoon to individual dessert dishes or arrange them attractively on a large platter. If you wish, you can place the halves on top of one another to resemble whole peaches. (Discard the syrup or save it to use for poaching fruit again.) Mask each of the peaches thoroughly with the *sauce cardinal*. Decorate the peaches with the *crème chantilly*. Then garnish them with whole raspberries if desired.

Crème Bavaroise à l'Orange

MOLDED ORANGE-FLAVORED CREAM

To serve 6 to 8

1 envelope plus 1 extra teaspoon
    unflavored gelatin
⅓ cup strained fresh orange
    juice
1 cup milk
5 egg yolks
¼ cup sugar

4 tablespoons Grand Marnier or
    Cointreau
1 tablespoon freshly grated orange
    peel
1½ cups chilled heavy cream
2 large navel oranges, divided into
    sections with the outside
    membranes peeled off
1 tablespoon sugar

Brush the inside of a 1-quart charlotte or ring mold with a film of vegetable oil, and invert the mold on paper towels to drain. In a heatproof measuring cup or small bowl, sprinkle the gelatin over the orange juice. When the gelatin has softened for 2 or 3 minutes, set the cup in a small skillet of simmering water and cook over low heat, stirring constantly, until the gelatin dissolves completely. Remove the skillet from the heat but leave the cup of gelatin and juice in the water to keep warm.

In a heavy 2- to 3-quart saucepan, scald the milk by heating it until bubbles begin to form around the edge of the pan; remove the pan from the heat. With a wire whisk, rotary or electric beater, beat the egg yolks and sugar together in a mixing bowl for 3 or 4 minutes, or until the yolks are pale yellow and slightly thickened. Stirring constantly, pour the hot milk in a thin stream over the egg yolks. When thoroughly blended, pour into a clean saucepan. Cook over low heat, stirring constantly, until the custard has thickened, and continue cooking until the custard coats the spoon like heavy cream. Do not let the custard come near the boiling point or it will curdle; if it seems to be getting too hot, lift the pan off the stove every few seconds to cool it. It must cook long enough, however, to thicken.

Remove the pan from the heat and stir in the dissolved gelatin and the orange juice. Strain the custard through a fine sieve into a large mixing bowl, and add 2 tablespoons of the Grand Marnier or Cointreau and the grated orange peel.

With a whisk, rotary or electric beater, whip the cream in a large chilled mixing bowl until it forms soft peaks. Set the bowl of custard into a pot or another, larger bowl filled with crushed ice or ice cubes and cold water. Stir the custard for 4 or 5 minutes, or until it is quite cold and begins to thicken. Beat thoroughly with a wire whisk to be sure it is perfectly smooth. Then scoop the whipped cream over the custard and use the rubber spatula to fold them together gently but thoroughly. Spoon the mixture into the oiled mold, cover tightly with plastic wrap or aluminum foil, and refrigerate for at least 3 hours, or until firm and set.

To unmold and serve the Bavarian cream, run a sharp knife around the sides of the mold and dip the bottom in hot water for a few seconds. Then wipe the outside of the mold dry, place a chilled serving plate upside down over the mold and, grasping both sides firmly, quickly turn the plate and mold over. Rap the plate on a table and the cream should slide easily out of the mold. If it doesn't unmold at once, repeat the whole process.

To garnish the Bavarian cream, sprinkle peeled orange sections with sugar and with the remaining Grand Marnier or Cointreau and arrange them attractively around the dessert.

Clafoutis aux Cerises

CHERRY CAKE

To serve 4 to 6

1½ cups milk
4 eggs
½ cup all-purpose flour
¼ cup sugar

2 teaspoons vanilla extract
2 to 3 cups fresh black sweet cherries, pitted; or drained, canned, pitted Bing cherries; or frozen sweet cherries, thawed and drained
Confectioners' (powdered) sugar

Preheat the oven to 350°. To make the batter in a blender, combine the milk, eggs, flour, sugar and vanilla in the blender jar, and whirl them at high speed for a few seconds. Turn the machine off and scrape down the sides of the jar with a rubber spatula, then blend again for about 40 seconds. To make the batter by hand, stir the flour and eggs together in a large mixing bowl, and slowly stir in the milk, sugar and vanilla extract. Beat with a whisk or a rotary or electric beater until the flour lumps disappear and the batter is smooth.

Pat the cherries completely dry with paper towels, then spread them evenly in a shallow, buttered baking dish or pan that holds 5 to 6 cups and is about 2 inches deep. Pour in the batter. Bake on the middle shelf of the oven for 1½ hours, or until the top is golden brown and firm to the touch. Dust lightly with confectioners' sugar, and serve the clafoutis while it is still warm.

Crêpes Soufflées au Citron
DESSERT CRÊPES WITH LEMON SOUFFLÉ FILLING

To serve 4 to 6 (about 2 each)

DESSERT CRÊPES
8 tablespoons butter (1 quarter-
  pound stick)
½ cup cold water

¼ cup milk
2 eggs plus 2 additional egg yolks
¾ cup unsifted all-purpose flour
1 tablespoon sugar
1 teaspoon freshly grated lemon peel
¼ teaspoon salt

DESSERT CRÊPES: First clarify the butter by melting it in a small, heavy saucepan or skillet over low heat, skimming off the surface foam. Spoon the clear butter on top into a bowl, and discard the milky solids at the bottom of the pan. Then make the batter for the *crêpes* in a blender or by hand with 2 tablespoons of the clarified butter, following the directions on page 10. After the batter has rested for at least 2 hours, cook the *crêpes* in the remaining clarified butter, using a 5-inch *crêpe* pan or heavy skillet with sloping sides, again following the directions on page 10. This recipe will make at least 12 *crêpes*. When the *crêpes* are finished, stack them on a plate. Set them aside, covered with plastic wrap.

LEMON SOUFFLÉ FILLING
3 tablespoons unsalted butter
5 level tablespoons sifted all-purpose
  flour
½ cup hot milk
3 egg yolks
4 tablespoons sugar

3 tablespoons strained fresh lemon
  juice
1 tablespoon freshly grated lemon
  peel
3 egg whites
Salt

LEMON SOUFFLÉ FILLING: Preheat the oven to 400°. In a heavy 1- to 2-quart saucepan, melt 3 tablespoons of butter over low heat, stir in the flour, then cook, stirring, for 1 to 2 minutes. Remove from the heat and let cool for a moment. Beat in the milk vigorously to blend *roux* and liquid. Cook, stirring constantly, until the mixture boils and thickens. Immediately scoop into a large bowl and beat in the egg yolks, one at a time. Add 3 tablespoons of the sugar, the lemon juice and finally the lemon peel, stirring thoroughly until all the ingredients are combined. In a separate bowl, beat the egg whites and a pinch of salt with a whisk or rotary beater until they cling to the beater; add the remaining 1 tablespoon of sugar and beat until the whites form stiff, unwavering peaks. With a rubber spatula, stir an overflowing tablespoon of egg white into the lemon soufflé base; then lightly fold in the rest of the egg whites.

Carefully separate the *crêpes* and lay them speckled side up on wax paper. Place about 1 tablespoon of the lemon soufflé mixture on the top half of each *crêpe* and gently lift the lower half up over it. Then lightly fold the *crêpes* into quarters to make small triangles. Arrange the *crêpes* side by side in a large, shallow, buttered baking dish. Sprinkle each *crêpe* with a little sugar, then bake them on the middle shelf of the oven for 10 minutes, or until they have puffed up and the sugar has melted to a light glaze. Serve the *crêpes* at once, on a heated platter or individual dessert plates.

Soufflé au Grand Marnier
ORANGE LIQUEUR SOUFFLÉ

To serve 4

2 tablespoons soft butter
3 tablespoons sugar
5 egg yolks
⅓ cup sugar
¼ cup Grand Marnier (1 two-ounce bottle)
1 tablespoon freshly grated orange peel
7 egg whites
¼ teaspoon cream of tartar
Confectioners' (powdered) sugar

Preheat the oven to 425°. Grease the bottom and sides of a 1½-quart soufflé dish with 2 tablespoons of soft butter. Sprinkle in 3 tablespoons of sugar, tipping and shaking the dish to spread the sugar evenly. Then turn the dish over and knock out the excess sugar. Set aside.

In the top of a double boiler, beat the egg yolks with a whisk, rotary or electric beater until they are well blended. Slowly add the sugar and continue beating until the yolks become very thick and pale yellow. Set the pan over barely simmering (not boiling) water and heat the egg yolks, stirring gently and constantly with a wooden spoon or rubber spatula, until the mixture thickens and becomes almost too hot to touch. Stir in the Grand Marnier and grated orange peel and transfer to a large bowl. Set the bowl into a pan filled with crushed ice or ice cubes and cold water, and stir the mixture until it is quite cold. Remove it from the ice.

In a large mixing bowl, preferably of unlined copper, beat the egg whites and the cream of tartar with a clean whisk or rotary beater until they form stiff, unwavering peaks. Using a rubber spatula, stir a large spoonful of beaten egg white into the egg-yolk mixture to lighten it. Gently fold the remaining egg whites into the mixture. Spoon the soufflé into the buttered, sugared dish, filling it to within 2 inches of the top. Smooth the top of the soufflé with the spatula. For a decorative effect, make a cap on the soufflé by cutting a trench about 1 inch deep 1 inch from the edge all around the top.

Bake on the middle shelf of the oven for 2 minutes, then reduce the heat to 400°. Continue baking for another 20 to 30 minutes, or until the soufflé has risen about 2 inches above the top of the mold and the top is lightly browned. Sprinkle with confectioners' sugar and serve it at once.

Mousse au Chocolat

CHOCOLATE MOUSSE

To serve 6 to 8

4 egg yolks
¼ cup superfine sugar
2 tablespoons Cognac
6 ounces semisweet chocolate, cut
   in small chunks

3 tablespoons strong coffee
8 tablespoons soft unsalted
   butter (1 quarter-pound stick),
   cut in ½-inch pieces
4 egg whites
½ cup heavy cream, whipped

Brush the inside of a 1-quart charlotte (cylindrical) or ring mold with a film of vegetable oil. Invert the mold on paper towels to drain.

In a heatproof mixing bowl, beat the egg yolks and sugar with a whisk, rotary or electric beater for 2 or 3 minutes, or until they are pale yellow and thick enough to form a ribbon when the whisk is lifted from the bowl. Beat in the Cognac.

Set the mixing bowl over a pan of barely simmering (not boiling) water, and continue beating for 3 or 4 minutes, or until the mixture is foamy and hot. Then set the bowl over a pan of iced water and beat for 3 or 4 minutes longer, or until the mixture is cool again and as thick and creamy as mayonnaise.

In a heavy 1- to 1½-quart saucepan set over low heat, or in the top of a double boiler over simmering water, melt the chocolate with the coffee, stirring constantly. When all the chocolate has dissolved, beat in the butter, one piece at a time, to make a smooth cream. Then beat the chocolate mixture into the egg yolks and sugar. In a separate bowl, with a clean whisk or beater, beat the egg whites until they are stiff enough to form stiff peaks on the wires of the whisk. Stir about one fourth of the egg whites into the chocolate mixture to lighten it, then very gently fold in the remaining egg whites. Spoon the mousse into the oiled mold or dessert cups, and refrigerate for at least 4 hours or until it has set.

To unmold and serve the *mousse au chocolat,* run a long, sharp knife around the sides of the mold and dip the bottom of it in hot water for a few seconds. Then wipe the outside of the mold dry, place a chilled serving plate upside down over the mold and, grasping both sides firmly, quickly turn the plate and mold over. Rap the plate on a table and the mousse should slide easily out of the mold. If the mousse doesn't unmold at once, repeat the whole process.

With a wire whisk, rotary or electric beater, whip the chilled cream in a large chilled bowl until it is firm enough to hold its shape softly. Garnish the mousse with the whipped cream.

Recipe Index: English

Hors d'Oeuvre

Cheese Fondue, French Style.................................. 3
Cheese Soufflé 6
Filled French Pancakes 10
French Oil and Vinegar Dressing............................ 16
French Omelet.. 16
Hollandaise.. 13
Hollandaise with Tarragon and White Wine.................. 14
Home-Style Pâté.. 14
Hot Anchovy Canapé 7
Marinated Vegetables, Greek Style.......................... 8
Mayonnaise 13
Mediterranean Vegetable Salad.............................. 5
Open-faced Cheese Tart 4
Open-faced Omelet with Peppers, Tomatoes and Ham 9
Sausage Baked in Pastry Crust.............................. 2
Sausage with French Potato Salad 12

Soups

Cream of Asparagus Soup.................................... 24
Cream of Mushroom Soup.................................... 26
French Onion Soup 21
Homemade Beef and Chicken Stocks......................... 18
Leek or Onion and Potato Soup............................. 22
Main-Course Meat and Cabbage Soup........................ 25
Mediterranean Fisherman's Soup with Hot Pepper Sauce 22
Oxtail Soup 17
Provençal Fish Soup with Garlic Mayonnaise 28
Purée of Carrot Soup....................................... 29
Split-Pea Soup 20
Vegetable Soup with Garlic, Basil and Tomato Sauce........ 19
White Bean Soup 27

Fish

Baked Fish with Spinach Stuffing.......................... 34
Broiled Salmon Steaks with Garlic and Herb Butter........ 35
Fillets of Sole with Mushroom and Wine Sauce 38
Fillets of Sole with White Wine Sauce 36
Lobster Simmered with Wine, Tomatoes and Herbs 39
Poached Bass with White Butter Sauce 30
Scallops Sautéed with Garlic Butter Sauce................. 33
Scallops with Mushrooms in White Wine Sauce.............. 32
Trout Sautéed in Butter.................................... 37

Poultry

Casserole Roasted Chicken with Vegetables................. 51
Chicken Simmered in Red Wine with Onions and Mushrooms... 52
Duck with Turnips.. 49
Old-fashioned Chicken Fricassee............................ 47
Roast Chicken 50
Roast Partridges on Liver Canapés......................... 46
Sautéed Chicken with Calvados (or Applejack) and Cream Sauce 44
Sautéed Chicken with Cream Sauce......................... 45
Sautéed Chicken with Shallots and Artichoke Hearts 43
Stuffed Chicken Simmered with Meat and Vegetables 41

Meat

Beef and Onions Braised in Beer 72
Beef Simmered with Vegetables 82
Beef Stew with Red Wine 54
Braised Pork Chops with Cream and Mustard Sauce 70
Braised Sauerkraut with Meat 79
Braised Shoulder of Lamb with White Beans 81
Braised Veal Chops with Ham and Parsley Dressing 64
Casserole of Tripe 78
Casserole of White Beans Baked with Meats 61
Casserole-roasted Veal 69
Glazed Roast Loin of Pork 80
Lamb Stew with Spring Vegetables 71
Loin Fillets of Pork with Prunes and Cream Sauce 57
Old-fashioned Veal Stew with Cream Sauce 74
Pork Chops Baked with Cabbage 66
Pot Roast of Beef Braised in Red Wine 58
Rabbit Stewed in White Wine Sauce 56
Roast Leg of Lamb 63
Sautéed Calf's Liver 75
Sautéed Kidneys with Mustard Sauce 67
Sautéed Steak with Red Wine Sauce 68
Sautéed Veal Scallops with Cream Sauce 77
Sweetbreads or Brains in Brown Butter Sauce 65
Veal Stew with Tomatoes and Mushrooms 76

Vegetables

Baked Stuffed Mushroom Caps 86
Boiled Artichokes 85
Boiled Asparagus 90
Braised Leeks 84
Braised Lettuce 95
Braised Red Cabbage in Red Wine with Chestnuts 89
Broiled Mushrooms 88
Crusty Molded Potatoes 93
Fresh Peas Braised with Onions and Lettuce 88
Glazed Carrots 92
Glazed White Onions 92
Green String Beans, Blanched and Buttered 89
Marinated Mushrooms 84
Mediterranean Vegetable Casserole 94
Scalloped Potatoes with Cheese 90
Tomatoes Baked with Bread Crumbs and Garlic 91

Desserts

Caramel Custard 102
Cherry Cake 105
Chocolate Mousse 108
Cream-Puff Pastry Ring with Whipped Cream Filling 97
Cream-Puff Pastry Rosettes 98
Dessert Crêpes with Lemon Soufflé Filling 106
Fresh Strawberry Tarts 96
Fruit Poached in Vanilla Syrup 99
Molded Custard with Glacéed Fruits 100
Molded Orange-flavored Cream 104
Orange Liqueur Soufflé 107
Pears Poached in Red Wine 101
Poached Peaches with Raspberry Purée 103

Recipe Index: French

Hors d'Oeuvre

Anchoyade 7
Crêpes Fourrées Gratinées 10
Fondue de Fromage 3
Légumes à la Grecque 8
Omelette 16
Pipérade 9
Quiche au Fromage 4
Salade Niçoise 5
Saucisson Chaud à la Lyonnaise 12
Saucisson en Croûte 2
Sauce Béarnaise 14
Sauce Hollandaise 13
Sauce Mayonnaise 13
Sauce Vinaigrette 16
Soufflé au Fromage 6
Terrine Maison 14

Soups

Bouillabaisse 22
Bourride 28
Fonds de Cuisine 18
Garbure 25
Potage Crécy 29
Potage Crème d'Asperges 24
Potage Crème de Champignons 26
Potage Parmentier; Vichyssoise 22
Potage Purée de Pois Cassés 20
Potage Purée Soissonnaise 27
Potage Queue de Boeuf 17
Soupe à l'Oignon 21
Soupe au Pistou 19

Fish

Bar Poché au Beurre Blanc 30
Coquilles Saint-Jacques à la Parisienne 32
Coquilles Saint-Jacques à la Provençale 33
Darnes de Saumon Grillés au Beurre d'Escargots . 35
Filets de Soles à la Parisienne, Gratinés 36
Filets de Soles Bonne Femme 38
Homard à l'Américaine 39
Poisson Farci à la Florentine 34
Truites à la Meunière 37

Poultry

Caneton aux Navets 49
Coq au Vin à la Bourguignonne 52
Fricassée de Poulet à l'Ancienne 47
Perdreaux Rôtis sur Canapés 46
Poule-au-pot 41
Poulet en Cocotte Bonne Femme 51
Poulet Rôti 50
Poulet Sauté à la Bordelaise 43
Poulet Sauté à la Crème 45
Poulet Sauté Vallée d'Auge 44

Meat

Bifteck Marchand de Vins 68
Blanquette de Veau à l'Ancienne 74
Boeuf Bourguignon 54
Boeuf à la Mode 58
Carbonades de Boeuf à la Flamande 72
Cassoulet 61
Choucroute Garnie 79
Côtes de Porc à l'Auvergnate 66
Côtes de Porc Braisées à la Moutarde 70
Côtes de Veau à l'Ardennaise 64
Épaule d'Agneau Braisée aux Haricots 81
Escalopes de Veau à la Savoyarde 77
Foie de Veau Sauté 75
Gigot d'Agneau Rôti 63
Navarin Printanier 71
Noisettes de Porc aux Pruneaux 57
Pot-au-feu 82
Ris de Veau ou Cervelles au Beurre Noir 65
Rognons en Casserole 67
Rôti de Porc Boulangère 80
Sauté de Lapin au Vin Blanc 56
Sauté de Veau Marengo 76
Tripes à la Mode de Caen 78
Veau Braisé en Casserole 69

Vegetables

Artichauts au Naturel 85
Asperges au Naturel 90
Carottes Glacées 92
Champignons Farcis 86
Champignons à la Grecque 84
Champignons Grillés 88
Chou Rouge à la Limousine 89
Haricots Verts au Naturel 89
Laitues Braisées 95
Oignons Glacés à Blanc 92
Petits Pois Frais à la Française 88
Poireaux Braisés 84
Pommes de Terre Anna 93
Pommes de Terre Dauphinoises 90
Ratatouille 94
Tomates à la Provençale 91

Desserts

Clafoutis aux Cerises 105
Compote de Fruits 99
Crème Bavaroise à l'Orange 104
Crème Caramel 102
Crêpes Soufflées au Citron 106
Diplomate 100
Mousse au Chocolat 108
Paris-Brest 97
Pêches Cardinal 103
Poires Pochées au Vin Rouge 101
Profiteroles 98
Soufflé au Grand Marnier 107
Tartes aux Fraises 96

Illustrations by Lionel Kalish   Printed in U.S.A.